ADB THROUGH THE DECADES

ADB'S FIRST DECADE (1966–1976)

ASIAN DEVELOPMENT BANK

50 YEARS

ADB

© 2016, 2017 Asian Development Bank
6 ADB Avenue, Mandaluyong City, 1550 Metro Manila, Philippines
Tel +63 2 632 4444; Fax +63 2 636 2444
www.adb.org; openaccess.adb.org

Some rights reserved. First edition 2016.
Updated edition 2017.

ISBN 978-92-9257-913-5 (Print), 978-92-9257-914-2 (e-ISBN)
Publication Stock No. TCS178965-2
DOI: http://dx.doi.org/10.22617/TCS178965-2

FOREWORD

The year 2016 marks the 50th anniversary of the Asian Development Bank (ADB). To commemorate this event, ADB has produced *ADB Through the Decades*, a series of volumes to provide a corporate chronicle over the past 5 decades of how ADB has evolved to engage its shareholders and other development partners in delivering financial and advisory services to its developing member countries in the Asia and Pacific region. Organized around key themes and topics for each decade, the series documents ADB's past work in such areas as strategic, operational, financial, and institutional developments.

The series synthesizes materials from many different sources, building from ADB's annual reports. The five volumes serve as decadal background notes for ADB's corporate history book, *Banking on the Future of Asia and the Pacific: 50 Years of the Asian Development Bank*, to be launched in 2017. Together, the history book and these volumes provide the first comprehensive corporate narrative on ADB's history since the previous ADB history book, *A Bank for Half the World*, was published in 1987.

Looking over the past 50 years, ADB has demonstrated a strong corporate continuity of being a multilateral development bank with an Asian character and global outreach. More significantly, the leadership of ADB has undertaken profound changes for the institution to stay relevant and responsive in serving the changing needs and expectations of its developing member countries. This spirit of change and innovation shall continue to drive ADB in the years ahead.

Reflecting on our history will give us a better insight for our work in the future. I hope that this *ADB Through the Decades* series becomes a key reference for ADB staff as well as other stakeholders from member countries, academic institutions, development partners, and civil society organizations.

TAKEHIKO NAKAO
December 2016

ACKNOWLEDGMENTS

This series, *ADB Through the Decades*, began as background research for the history book project chronicling the first 50 years of the Asian Development Bank (ADB). In the last 50 years, ADB has continuously evolved in response to dynamic changes across the Asia and Pacific region. The story of ADB's transformation became evident as the team tasked to support the ADB corporate history book project sifted through ADB's annual reports, past and present President's speeches, official and personal correspondences, loan documents, policy and strategy papers, evaluation reports, transcripts of interviews, historical records, and other archival materials. Drawing from the rich but fragmented sources of information, the team prepared background notes for each decade as an effort to capture and synthesize the significant developments and key turning points in ADB's history.

President Takehiko Nakao encouraged the team to publish the series as a stand-alone reference to a wider audience, including ADB staff. This work was done in parallel with the drafting of the ADB history book and took more than 2 years to complete. What were intended as internal supporting documents for the history book project in the end became five volumes that comprise the *ADB Through the Decades* series. This series provides the first comprehensive institutional record of the different facets of ADB's work—strategic, operational, financial, and organizational—spanning 50 years of ADB's history.

The first four volumes of the series were led by Valerie Hill, Director of the Strategy, Policy and Business Process Division (SPBP), Strategy, Policy and Review Department (SPD) with Edeena Pike, Strategy and Policy Specialist, Office of the Director General, SPD. The fifth volume was led by Ananya Basu, Principal Economist at the Pacific Department (PARD). Jade Tolentino, Research Consultant, provided substantive analytical support on all the volumes. Xianbin Yao, Director General, PARD, provided overall guidance and shared his insights on ADB's history to further enrich the notes. Peter McCawley, main author of the ADB history book, gave useful comments throughout the process.

This series benefited from comments and suggestions received from various departments and offices, as well as thematic and sector groups across ADB, during the interdepartmental review process. The volumes received written contributions from an interdepartmental focal group composed of Kinzang Wangdi (Budget, Personnel, and Management Systems Department [BPMSD]); Shanny Campbell and Noriko Sato (Central and West Asia Department); David Kruger (Department of External Relations [DER]); David Sobel (East Asia Department); Jesus Felipe and Juzhong Zhuang (Economic Research and Regional Cooperation Department [ERCD]); Medardo Abad, Jr. (Office of Administrative Services [OAS]); Nariman Mannapbekov (formerly of the Office of the Secretary [OSEC]); Emma Veve (Pacific Department [PARD]); Kiyoshi Taniguchi (Private Sector Operations Department [PSOD]) and Elsie Araneta (formerly of PSOD); Hiranya Mukhopadhyay (South Asia Department); Jason Rush (Southeast Asia Department); K. E. Seetharam (Sustainable Development and Climate Change Department [SDCC]) and Roshan Shahay (formerly of SDCC); and Mina Oh (Treasury Department [TD]).

Access to important historical records and data was vital in completing the *ADB Through the Decades* series. Technical inputs were provided by SPD (Vanessa Dimaano, Marvin de Asis, Socorro Regalado, and Grace Sevilla); Controller's Department (Setijo Boentaran and Lani Gomez); TD (Fean Asprer); BPMSD (Melanie dela Cruz and Kingzang Wangdi); and ERCD (Kaushal Joshi, Rana Hasan, Arturo Martinez, Pilipinas Quising, and Editha Lavina) in vetting the data used. The discussions on financial matters were largely drawn from the specialized report commissioned by TD on *A History of Financial Management at the Asian Development Bank*. Excellent support was extended by the OAS Records and Archives Unit (Medardo Abad, Jr., Richard Dimalanta, and Heidi Dizon) and Library Services (Marilyn Rosete and Voltere Serraon), who were always quick and resourceful in sourcing and screening historical photos and institutional documents; and OSEC (Nathaniel Casuncad, Genedyn Ebreo), who were ready to assist in Board document retrieval.

Overall production was supervised by Edeena Pike. DER (Robert Hugh Davis and Cynthia Hidalgo) helped in managing the volumes' production, particularly at the initial stages. Cherry Lynn Zafaralla was the copyeditor of the five volumes as well as publication coordinator. Joe Mark Ganaban provided the layout, graphics design, and typesetting, and Anthony Victoria of DER conceptualized the covers and box packaging design. Rowena Agripa, Lorena Catap, Esmeralda Fulgentes, Ma. Carolina Faustino-Chan, and Sharlene Guinto provided administrative assistance at various stages. Finally, the Logistics Management Unit of OAS (Razel Gonzaga and Wyn Lauzon) provided indispensable assistance in the printing of the volumes.

CONTENTS

TABLES, FIGURES, AND BOXES

ABBREVIATIONS

AAS	–	Asian Agricultural Survey
ADB	–	Asian Development Bank
ADF	–	Asian Development Fund
ASF	–	Agricultural Special Fund
BOD	–	Board of Directors
DFI	–	development finance institution
DMC	–	developing member country
ECAFE	–	Economic Commission for Asia and the Far East
GCI	–	general capital increase
GDP	–	gross domestic product
ICT	–	information and communication technology
MPSF	–	Multipurpose Special Fund
OCR	–	ordinary capital resources
OPEC	–	Organization of the Petroleum Exporting Countries
RETA	–	regional technical assistance
TA	–	technical assistance
TASF	–	Technical Assistance Special Fund

DATA NOTES

L ending approvals data used in the five volumes in this series, *ADB Through the Decades*, refer to loan, grant, equity investment, and guarantee approvals of the Asian Development Bank (ADB). They include sovereign and nonsovereign operations of ADB from 1967 to 2016. Approvals include ADB-funded lending operations from ordinary capital resources (OCR) and the Asian Development Fund. Cofinancing resources are discussed separately in the section "Financial Policies and Mobilization Efforts."

For both lending and technical assistance (TA) operations, regional breakdown is based on current member economy groupings of ADB. Central and West Asia includes Afghanistan, Armenia, Azerbaijan, Georgia, Kazakhstan, the Kyrgyz Republic, Pakistan, Tajikistan, Turkmenistan, and Uzbekistan. East Asia is composed of the People's Republic of China; Hong Kong, China; the Republic of Korea; Mongolia; and Taipei,China. South Asia covers Bangladesh, Bhutan, India, Maldives, Nepal, and Sri Lanka. Southeast Asia includes Brunei Darussalam, Cambodia, Indonesia, the Lao People's Democratic Republic, Malaysia, Myanmar, the Philippines, Singapore, Thailand, and Viet Nam. Finally, the Cook Islands, Fiji, Kiribati, the Marshall Islands, the Federated States of Micronesia, Nauru, Palau, Papua New Guinea, Solomon Islands, Timor-Leste, Tonga, Tuvalu, and Vanuatu comprise the Pacific developing member countries.

Lending data were sourced from two ADB databases, which use slightly different methodologies in recording project information. The operational approvals from 1967 to 1996 (volumes 1–3) were culled from the ADB loan, technical assistance, grant, and equity approvals database, which excludes terminated instruments (loans, grants, equity investments, and guarantees that were approved but terminated before their signing date). This database uses ADB's old sector classification system. Meanwhile, the operational approvals from 1997 to 2016 (volumes 4 and 5) were downloaded from ADB's Suite of Strategy 2020 Report of eOperations database which records gross approvals and follows a new project sector classification. All data are as of 31 December 2016.

Technical assistance operations data refer to TA approvals funded by the Technical Assistance Special Fund and Japan Special Fund only. For the first four volumes, the sources for the data are the loan, technical assistance, grant, and equity approvals database (as of 31 December 2016.); and for the fifth volume, ADB's Operations Planning and Coordination Division, Strategy, Policy and Review Department.

Staff information include management, international, and national and administrative staff. They include director's advisors and assistants, staff on special leave without pay, and on secondment status. Staff data are sourced from ADB's Budget, Personnel, and Management Systems Department, and may not tally with the numbers from ADB's annual reports, which used different classifications of staff data.

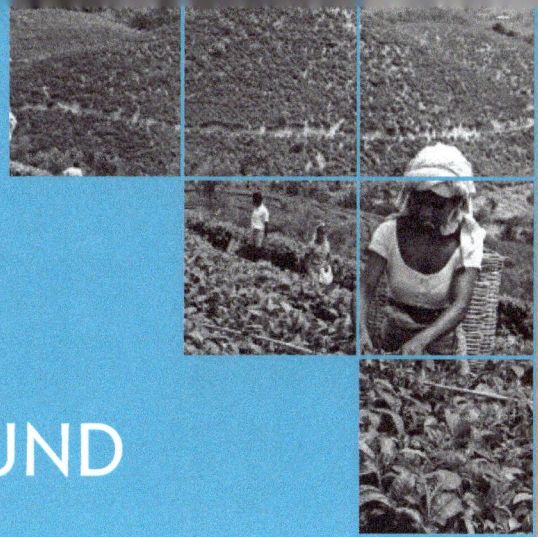

I. REGIONAL BACKGROUND

- In the mid-1960s, Asia and the Pacific was the poorest region in the world.
- Worldwide inflation, sharp increases in oil prices, a persistent economic recession in the industrialized world, and worsening terms of trade challenged the region in the second half of the decade.
- Toward the end of the decade, policy responses of developing member countries, together with more favorable international developments, significantly altered the economic situation and gave way to a sense of self-assurance and optimism in the region.

When ADB was established, Asia and the Pacific had an annual per capita income of about $100, significantly below that of the Latin America and Sub-Saharan Africa regions. Its population of 1.7 billion was more than three times that of Sub-Saharan Africa and Latin America combined (Table 1).[1] One of the most important challenges facing many countries in the region was how to feed this large and growing population. Although the region was composed of countries with widely different levels of development, they also shared common features. Many were adjusting to political and economic independence from their former ruler. Their economies were predominantly agricultural, and trade, where exports were mainly primary commodities, was limited. While the Green Revolution was under way, many attempts at food self-sufficiency were hampered by high population growth rates, limited agricultural technology, and natural disasters. Some sought industrialization as a possible solution, relying on export-led industry as a means to expand their economic base, generate employment, and earn foreign exchange. However, capital for investment and basic infrastructure was lacking.

The second half of the first decade brought a new set of problems for ADB's developing member countries (DMCs), problems largely beyond their

---

[1] See Appendix Tables A1.1 and A1.2 on selected economic and social indicators of the region.

Table 1: Population and Gross Domestic Product, Selected Regional Groupings, 1966–2015

Regions	1966	1976	1986	1996	2006	2015
Developing Asia						
GDP ($ billion)	163	426	1,014	2,937	6,412	18,063
Population (million)	1,718	2,173	2,626	3,124	3,555	3,903
GDP per capita ($)	95	196	386	940	1,804	4,628
Share of world GDP (%)	8	7	7	9	13	25
Share of world population (%)	51	52	53	54	54	53
Asia's share of world GDP (constant, 2010 $) (%)	14	16	19	24	25	31
Latin America and Caribbean (excluding high-income economies)						
GDP ($ billion)	117	411	706	1,894	3,030	4,855
Population (million)	244	314	392	471	544	605
GDP per capita ($)	481	1,306	1,800	4,024	5,569	8,020
Share of world GDP (%)	6	6	5	6	6	7
Share of world population (%)	7	8	9	11	13	15
Sub-Saharan Africa (excluding high-income economies)						
GDP ($ billion)	42	142	235	348	798	1,571
Population (million)	264	342	454	600	783	1,001
GDP per capita ($)	158	416	518	581	1,019	1,570
Share of world GDP (%)	2	2	2	1	2	2
Share of world population (%)	8	8	9	10	12	14

GDP = gross domestic product.
Notes: Gross domestic product is expressed in current $ billion. Developing Asia includes developing member economies of ADB. Asia includes ADB's regional developing and developed members (Australia, Japan, and New Zealand).
Source: The World Bank. World Development Indicators. http://data.worldbank.org/indicator/NY.GDP.MKTP.CD (accessed 7 December 2016).

control. Just as many countries were starting to show encouraging progress in economic development, they experienced severe setbacks through a train of adverse developments on the international economic front. The combination of worldwide inflation, sharp increases in oil prices, a persistent economic recession in the industrialized world, and worsening terms of trade slowed down economic and social progress and reduced the earlier momentum of growth. War and natural disasters also took a heavy toll. In 1973, the Organization of the Petroleum Exporting Countries (OPEC) raised petroleum prices by 20%. All but two of ADB's DMCs (Indonesia and Malaysia) were net oil importers. The oil price hike accelerated inflation and adversely affected production, consumption, and external payments. Moreover, higher oil import bills forced industrialized countries to reduce commodity imports, causing commodity prices to fall to the further detriment of DMCs. Many countries borrowed short-term commercial funds to finance their balance of payment deficits, thereby shouldering heavy debt service burdens.

The DMCs responded to the crisis in a variety of ways. In most DMCs, sluggish industrial production led to reduced employment. To alleviate hardships, measures were undertaken such as price controls, rationing of essential consumer goods, tax relief for the poor, and employment-generating expenditures. More intensive efforts were made to mobilize savings through higher interest rates on bank deposits. Trade policies sought to improve export performance and reduce the growth of imports. Many DMCs adopted tighter monetary and credit policies to dampen inflation and discourage hoarding of essential goods. Most DMCs had to rely more heavily on budgetary deficits to meet their rapidly expanding current and investment expenditures.

Together with favorable international developments, the different policies pursued by DMCs paved the way for a better economic landscape by the end of the decade. At the same time, the end of hostilities in Viet Nam in 1975 brought to the fore massive problems of reconstruction, rehabilitation, and reintegration.

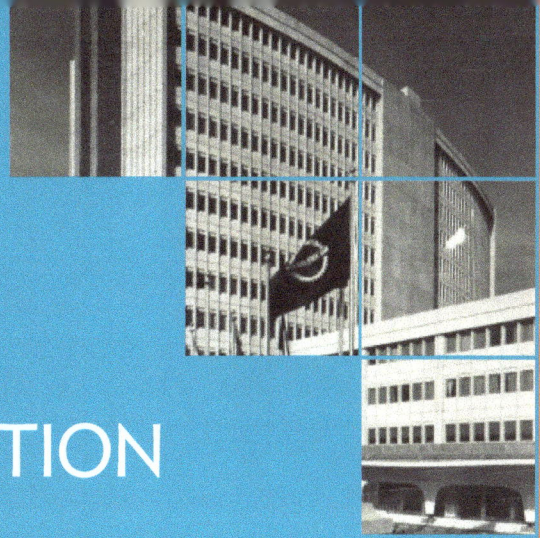

II. BIRTH OF AN INSTITUTION

- The rise of nationalism led to independence for many countries in the region after the Second World War.
- The 1960s ushered a new spirit of increasing regionalism among nations. One particular idea that began to gain strength was that the relatively weak individual countries of Asia and the Pacific should work together to reduce economic dependency on Europe and North America.
- ADB itself was conceived to foster economic growth in the region, both collectively and individually.

There is ambiguity as to who first thought of the idea of an Asian development bank. As early as 1956, Japanese Finance Minister Hisato Ichimada suggested the establishment of a new financial agency for Southeast Asia. This was followed by an announcement a year later from the Japanese Prime Minister Nobusuke Kishi on a proposal to create an "Asian Commercial Fund" to provide long-term, low-interest loans to Asian developing countries.[2] Lacking wider international support, these ideas did not materialize at the time.

Outside Japan, Premier Solomon Bandaranaike of Sri Lanka (formerly Ceylon) mentioned the possibility of establishing a regional development bank in 1959 but he was assassinated before he could develop this idea further. In 1962, an independent suggestion was made in writing by a Ceylonese banker, C. Loganathan, who was invited to contribute a paper to an Asian Banker's seminar in 1962, and who chose the topic "Regional Economic Cooperation in Asia: A Case for a Development Bank for Countries of the United Nations Economic Commission for Asia and the Far East (ECAFE)." The paper was never submitted, as the seminar was cancelled because of the outbreak of fighting between India and Pakistan.

At around the same time, a Japanese economic journalist, Kaoru Ohashi, who headed a private research institute in Tokyo, put together a group of friends to discuss the idea. They started meeting monthly from October 1962 onward. Takeshi Watanabe, former Executive Director for Japan at the World Bank and International Monetary Fund, joined the group in February

---

[2]   For further details, see P. W. Huang, Jr. 1975. *The Asian Development Bank: Diplomacy and Development in Asia*. New York.

1963, which was composed of other Ministry of Finance officials and Japanese bankers. By August 1963, the group had drafted a brief paper entitled "A Private Plan for the Establishment of the Asian Development Bank" in which they concluded that a $1 billion regional development bank was needed to supplement the World Bank's activities in Asia. The United States (US) should participate so that the bank would not appear to be dominated by Japan. However, the US at that time was not fully convinced about joining, while Japan (certain that the initiative to create a development bank for Asia would come from other Asian economies) decided it was appropriate to take a low-key approach and wait for an invitation.

In July 1963, a young Thai banker, Paul Sithi-Amnuai, independently elaborated on the idea in a paper for ECAFE entitled "The Case for a Regional Bank for the ECAFE Region—with Special Reference to the Development of Intra-Regional Trade." In September 1963, ECAFE convened a working group of experts on regional economic cooperation. In December 1963, at the first Ministerial Conference on Asian Economic Cooperation held by ECAFE in Manila, a resolution was passed, endorsing a proposal to establish a regional development bank

for Asia. In October 1964, ECAFE was instructed to assemble a group of experts to begin the task of translating the idea into reality.[3] Takeshi Watanabe, who would later become ADB's first President, was invited to join this panel of experts.

In March 1965, ECAFE set up a consultative committee to elicit members' views and prepare a draft agreement establishing a regional development bank, which was adopted at the second ECAFE ministerial conference held in November 1965 in Manila.[4]

It was also during this meeting that members decided on Manila as the head office of this regional bank.[5] During the meeting, 22 governments signed the *Articles of Agreement Establishing the Asian Development Bank* (Box 1), which remained open until end-January 1966. Another nine countries signed it afterward in Bangkok. The agreement entered into force on 22 August 1966 with the ratification or acceptance of 15 signatories, paving the way for the establishment of the Asian Development Bank (ADB).

Table 2 provides the chronology of events leading to the establishment of ADB.

Box 1: The Charter of the Asian Development Bank

The overall purpose, functions, and operating principles of the Asian Development Bank (ADB) are enshrined in the *Articles of Agreement Establishing the Asian Development Bank*, also known as the ADB Charter. The first ADB President, Takeshi Watanabe, in his address at the 1968 ADB Annual Meeting, referred to the ADB Charter as the Bank's "institutional heartbeat." The ADB Charter laid down the vision of ADB "to foster economic growth and cooperation in the region and to contribute to the acceleration of the process of economic development of the developing member countries in the region, collectively and individually." It further articulated that "to fulfill its purpose, the Bank will give priority to those regional, subregional as well as national projects and programs, which will contribute most effectively to the harmonious economic growth of the region as a whole, and having special regard to the needs of the smaller or less developed member countries in the region" (Article 1, ADB Charter). It also gave a unique character to the Bank as "Asian in its basic character," yet owned by both regional and nonregional membership in a spirit of international cooperation and partnership. The ADB Charter has endured and has never been amended to date.

Source: ADB. 1966. *Agreement Establishing the Asian Development Bank*. Manila.

---

[3] For a brief account on the role of ECAFE on ADB's establishment from 1963 to 1966, see R. Krishnamurti. 1997. *The Seeding Days*. Manila: ADB.

[4] A staff from Japan's Ministry of Finance, Tadao Chino, was seconded to the ECAFE Consultative Committee. He would eventually become the seventh President of ADB in 1999.

[5] The selection of a site for ADB's permanent headquarters proved to be a difficult issue. It had been agreed that only regional members would vote. The candidates were: Bangkok, Colombo, Kabul, Kuala Lumpur, Manila, Phnom Penh, Singapore, Teheran, and Tokyo. Initially, there were eight votes for Tokyo, four for Teheran, and three for Manila. The other candidates with only one vote each withdrew. At a second ballot held the next morning, Tokyo remained ahead with eight votes followed by Manila with six votes, and Teheran with four. Teheran withdrew. Manila eventually won at the final ballot with nine votes to Tokyo's eight. For further details, see T. Watanabe. 1973. *Towards a New Asia: Memoirs of the First President of the Asian Development Bank*. Manila: ADB. pp. 14–16.

Table 2: Establishment of ADB—Chronology of Official Meetings

Date/Year	Venue	Highlights
1963		
5–18 March	Manila	**Economic Commission for Asia and the Far East, 19th session** A resolution recommended adoption of accelerated measures for regional economic cooperation. The executive secretary of the Economic Commission in Asia and the Far East (ECAFE), U Nyun, called for the preparation of a high-level meeting later in the year.
15 August–13 September	Bangkok	**Working Group of Experts on Regional Economic Cooperation** The expert group on regional cooperation (convened by ECAFE's executive secretary) proposed the establishment of an Asian development bank.
21–26 October	Bangkok	**Preparatory Meeting for the First Ministerial Conference on Asian Economic Cooperation** Ministers from the Asian region met to discuss the expert group's recommendations. It was proposed that another expert group be constituted to study the matter and report its findings to ECAFE.
3–6 December	Manila	**First Ministerial Conference for Asian Economic Cooperation** Two resolutions were passed: endorsing the establishment of a regional development bank for Asia; and requesting the ECAFE executive secretary to undertake the necessary investigations and recommend the institutional arrangements needed to establish the bank.
1964		
2–17 March	Tehran	**ECAFE, 20th session** By February, R. Krishnamurti, chief of ECAFE's International Trade Division, organized a panel of experts. ECAFE's 20th session in March endorsed the establishment of the Asian Development Bank, otherwise to be known as ADB or the Bank.
20–31 October	Bangkok	**Expert Group on ADB** Ten members of ECAFE's working group of experts met formally for the first time, including Japan's Takeshi Watanabe. They discussed major issues (purpose and character of the Bank, capitalization, membership, etc.). Conclusions of the group were circulated to ECAFE member governments.
1965		
16–29 March	Wellington	**ECAFE, 21th session** A resolution was passed requesting the ECAFE executive secretary to give top priority to the ADB project and convene a high-level consultative committee to study the matter. The consultative committee was directed to report to the upcoming Second Ministerial Conference on Asian Economic Cooperation.
23 June–4 August	Bangkok	**Consultative Committee on ADB** The nine-member consultative committee held its first meeting on 23 June. Japan and the United States would announce their planned monetary contribution ($200 million each). The committee embarked on a tour around the world to solicit support for the project.
21 October–1 November	Bangkok	**Preparatory Committee on ADB** A preparatory committee composed of 31 regional and nonregional countries met and took final decisions on the Bank's goals and structures. The ADB Charter was finalized.
29 November–1 December	Manila	**Second Ministerial Conference on Asian Economic Cooperation** Membership of countries and the amount of their subscriptions were formalized. After three voting rounds, Manila was selected as the site of the Bank's headquarters.
2–4 December	Manila	**Conference of Plenipotentiaries on ADB** Twenty-two governments signed the Charter during the Manila meeting in December 1965; another nine countries signed before the prescribed deadline of 31 January 1966 (Bangkok meeting). A committee was set up and instructed to "initiate, devise and undertake the necessary steps for the establishment of the Bank, including the preparation for the Inaugural Meeting of the Board of Governors for the Bank."
1966		
28 January–21 November	Bangkok, Manila, and Tokyo	**Committee on Preparatory Arrangements for the Establishment of ADB** The committee on preparatory arrangements for the establishment of ADB met for several days on five occasions. A report was completed in November for submission to the inaugural meeting in Tokyo.
24–26 November	Tokyo	**Inaugural Meeting of the Board of Governors of ADB** Takeshi Watanabe was unanimously elected President of the Bank. A resolution was passed increasing the Bank's authorized capital from its original $1 billion to $1.1 billion. Ten members of the ADB Board of Directors were elected: seven representing regional members, and three representing nonregional members.
19 December	Manila	**Opening Ceremonies of ADB** Representatives from the Bank's 31 members gathered at the site of the Bank's temporary headquarters in Manila for the opening ceremonies.

Sources: Chalkley. 1977. *Asian Development Bank: A Decade of Progress*. Manila: ADB. pp.50-53; P. W. Huang. 1975. *The Asian Development Bank: Diplomacy and Development in Asia*. New York: Vantage Press. pp. 1-109; R. Krishnamurti, 1977. *ADB: The Seeding Days*. Manila: ADB. p.1; and D. T. Yasutomo. 1983. *Japan and the Asian Development Bank*. New York: Praeger, p. 31.

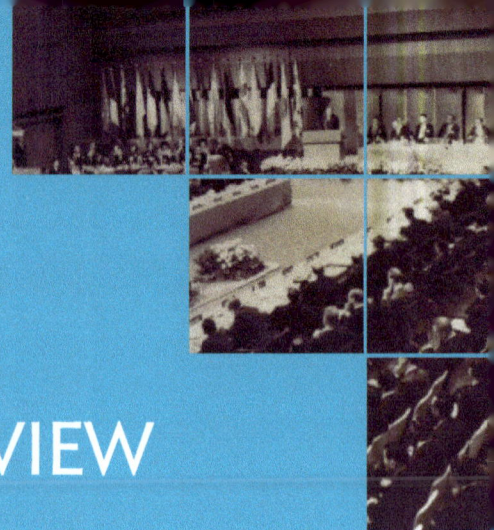

III. INSTITUTIONAL OVERVIEW

- The inaugural meeting of the Board of Governors was held on 24–26 November 1966 in Tokyo. Takeshi Watanabe was elected as ADB's first President.
- ADB formally opened for business in Manila on 19 December 1966, with 31 members (20 regional and 11 nonregional).
- Unlike other regional development banks that were established earlier, Asian countries felt that ADB membership should be open to countries outside the region so that ADB could raise loans in the world capital markets.

A. Membership, Capital Base, and Voting Power

By end-September 1966, 30 economies had satisfied conditions for membership and remitted their first installment of paid-in capital subscriptions. These included Afghanistan; Australia; Austria; Belgium; Cambodia; Canada; Denmark; Finland; Germany; India; Italy; Japan; the Republic of Korea; the Lao People's Democratic Republic (Lao PDR); Malaysia; Nepal; the Netherlands; New Zealand; Norway; Pakistan; the Philippines; Samoa (formerly Western Samoa); Singapore; Sri Lanka; Sweden; Taipei,China; Thailand; the United Kingdom; the United States (US); and Viet Nam. Indonesia became the 31st member during the inaugural meeting of the Board of Governors.

At its inception in 1966, ADB's main source of funds was its members' capital subscription payments. Out of the initial capitalization of $1 billion, Japan and the US were the biggest shareholders, offering to contribute $200 million each (equivalent to over 20% of subscribed capital and 17% of total voting power). The third was India with 9.6% of subscribed capital and 8.3% of voting power, followed by Australia with 8.8% of subscribed capital and 7.6% of voting power. The capitalization was increased to $1.1 billion during the inaugural meeting to accommodate initial subscriptions of potential new members. Over the next 10 years, ADB would welcome 11 new members: Switzerland (1967); Hong Kong, China (1969); Fiji and France (1970); Papua New Guinea (1971); Tonga (1972); Bangladesh, Myanmar, and Solomon Islands (1973); Kiribati (1974); and the Cook Islands (1976). By the end of the first decade, ADB had 42 members (29 regional and 13 nonregional). As more countries joined ADB, and as certain members agreed to raise their subscription, ADB's subscribed capital rose to $2 billion in 1972 and $3 billion by 1973. By end-1976, the members had subscribed $3.7 billion (an overall increase of 178%), with paid-in capital equivalent to $1.2 billion (or 32% of subscribed capital).[6] This reflected a general increase in the capital stock of 150% in 1972, and special capital increases for three regional members (the Republic of Korea, twice in 1973 and 1975, as well as Indonesia and Malaysia, both in 1975) and two nonregional members (Canada and Germany, both in 1976). A second capital increase of 135% was approved by the Board of Governors in 1976.

From the very beginning, Asian countries felt that ADB membership should be open to countries outside the region. In adopting this outward-looking approach, they recognized the value of cooperation with non-Asian developed countries so that ADB could raise loans in the world capital markets. However, the Charter required that 60% of total capital be contributed by regional members, consistent with the provision under the ADB Charter for the institution to be "Asian in its basic character." The original capital subscriptions of regional members were determined by a formula that took into account the gross domestic product (GDP) per capita of each country, its tax revenue, and its exports. For nonregional members, their subscriptions were negotiated.[7] The allocation of votes was made within these two separate categories of member countries. Every member was entitled to a "basic vote" regardless of the size of their contribution or regional status. Basic votes constituted 20% of total votes, a provision made to protect the interest of smaller countries. In addition, members had one vote per share subscribed. Proportional votes were divided from the remaining 80% (with 40% of this amount for nonregional and 60% for regional members) in amounts corresponding to their relative share of capital subscriptions. New members therefore diluted the shares of current members. By the end of the first decade, Japan and the US each held 16.4% of subscribed capital and 13.6% of voting power.

B. Organizational Matters, Internal Resources, and Staffing

1. First President

During the first session of the inaugural meeting of ADB's Board of Governors held on 24–26 November 1966 in Tokyo, Japan, Takeshi Watanabe was elected as ADB's first President. He would serve in this capacity for 6 years until 1972 (Box 2). As stipulated in the ADB Charter (Article 34, para. 5), the President shall act as chief of staff and conduct the day-to-day business of the Bank, under the direction of the Board of Directors.

As ADB President, Watanabe took it upon himself to visit all member countries to familiarize himself with the prevailing economic climate in each country, listen to their views regarding the operations of ADB, and secure competent personnel as staff. He also used this opportunity to discuss his vision for ADB. First, President Watanabe envisioned ADB's role as the "family doctor" of Asian countries, which should know the health histories of every member of the family and be ready to give advice on any problem (Box 3). Second, ADB should be a bank, and not an aid agency. As such, it should apply strict standards in appraising projects and keeping its financial management in good order.[8]

---

[6] Subscribed capital is divided into two parts: amounts to be paid to ADB, and those that are callable from the countries but in fact are maintained in the member countries until needed. The callable amount serves to guarantee ADB loans and bonds in the world capital markets. These terms were designed to make it easier for countries to pay the amounts pledged.

[7] Nonregional subscriptions had to reach a minimum of $5 million. Only developed countries were allowed to join from outside Asia.

[8] T. Watanabe, 1973. *Towards a New Asia: Memoirs of the First President of the Asian Development Bank*. Manila: ADB. pp. 36–37.

Box 2: First ADB President Takeshi Watanabe
(24 November 1966–24 November 1972)

Takeshi Watanabe was 60 when he was elected as the first President of the Asian Development Bank (ADB). Born on 15 February 1906 in Tokyo, Japan, he was the son of the late Minister of Justice, Viscount Chifuyu Watanabe, and the grandson of the late Minister of Finance, Viscount Kunitake Watanabe. A graduate of Tokyo Imperial University Law School with a degree in political science, President Watanabe joined Japan's Ministry of Finance in 1930, where he served for 21 years before being appointed ambassador to St. James Court in London in 1952. After that he served as Japan's representative to the World Bank and International Monetary Fund. He retired to private life in 1960 as financial consultant. In this capacity, he worked for the metropolitan governments of Tokyo and Osaka in connection with their flotation of foreign bonds in the European and United States (US) markets. He reentered government service in 1965 as a member of the expert panel to help form ADB. President Watanabe played a pivotal role in moving ADB from an idea into reality and is considered by many as the "father" of ADB.

As President, Watanabe participated in various international conferences and toured many prospective member countries as the chief promoter of ADB. During his tenure, he combined idealism with practicality, and toughness with compassion. Under his leadership during ADB's formative years, he initially focused on the administrative, organizational, and funding challenges of establishing a new bank. Regional surveys were also undertaken to develop a fuller understanding of the social and economic conditions of ADB's developing member countries. ADB approved its first loan on 23 January 1968, just a little more than a year after it had started business.

During President Watanabe's 6-year term, ADB approved 117 loans totaling over $950 million. It negotiated its first general capital increase (GCI) and made its name in the European, Japanese, and US markets. Watanabe was reelected as President for a second term during the fourth ADB Annual Meeting held in April 1971 in Singapore. Just 4 months into his second term, he suffered a hemorrhage in a retina.

His doctors advised him to slow down and he announced his intention to resign in May 1972. His resignation became effective in November 1972, after which President Watanabe took on a number of roles, including adviser to the Bank of Tokyo and President of the Japan Credit Rating Agency. His book, *Towards a New Asia: Memoirs of the First President of the Asian Development Bank*, was published in 1973. He passed away in Japan on 23 August 2010 at the age of 104.

Sources: D. Wilson. 1987. *A Bank for Half the World: The Story of the Asian Development Bank*. Manila; other ADB sources.

Box 3: ADB as a Family Doctor

In a world populated with aggressive, older institutions, the Asian Development Bank (ADB) has acquired a clear, unmistakable identity of its own. This did not happen by accident. As President, Takeshi Watanabe clearly stated during ADB's Inaugural Meeting in Tokyo, in spite of its infancy, ADB does not wish to be spoon-fed or carried on the back of others. Such identity was reinforced by the image of ADB that President Watanabe worked hard to project to its member countries. The first image he chose was that of a "close friend of the Asian family of nations, a friend conversant with their problems and always close at hand to provide sincere and understanding counsel."

That image would then be refined into that of a "family doctor." Like an Oriental family doctor, ADB is eclectic and deeply pragmatic. To the problems each Asian country has to face, ADB provides not intellectualized or rationalized answers, but rather positive and practical down-to-earth solutions, taking the lives of nations simply as they are, with all their individual complexities, confusions, incompatibilities, and contradictions. Because of this, the Bank follows an empirical and inductive style. Instead of approaching from the general to the particular, from overall planning to specific projects, ADB prefers to start with individual projects, to increase its knowledge from practical experience on the ground.

Depending on the circumstances, ADB does not hesitate to change priorities or objectives. Its empirical approach has been tempered by intuition and a grasp for nuance. This was illustrated by the special attention President Watanabe attached to the creation of an atmosphere of cooperation and trust between ADB and its beneficiary nations. President Watanabe stressed that it was essential to learn before teaching, and to avoid an attitude of teaching the ignorant.

Source: B. Hoan. 1972. Farewell Speech in Honor of President Watanabe 23 November. Manila: ADB.

2. Board of Governors

In addition to electing the first President, the inaugural ADB Board of Governors approved the Report of the Committee on Preparatory Arrangements for the Establishment of ADB, including the draft headquarters agreement with the Philippine government; the by-laws of the Bank; and the Report of the Secretary-General of the United Nations as Depository of the ADB Charter.

3. Board of Directors

Ten executive directors (seven regional and three nonregional) were also appointed during the inaugural meeting of the Board of Governors. They were Cornelio Balmaceda (Philippines), Helmut Abramowski (Germany), Byung Kyu Chun (Republic of Korea), J. M. Garland (Australia), Ng Kam Poh (Malaysia), P.V.R. Rao (India), Khouw Bian Tie (Indonesia), Wilfred Kenneth Wardroper (Canada), Bernard Zagorin (US), and Masaru Fukuda (Japan). The Board, to be based permanently in Manila, met four times during 1966, and 36 times in 1967, equivalent to an average of three meetings per month. Its deliberations in the first year focused mostly on the organization of ADB, staff regulations, and administrative matters. To facilitate better representation of the growing membership, the strength of the Board of Directors (BOD) was increased from 10 to 12 (eight regional and four nonregional) in 1969. Constituencies were rearranged as a result (Box 4).

4. Organizational Structure

The first organizational structure of ADB was designed to meet the principles of simplicity, efficiency, and economy. The institution was initially organized into eight departments and offices (Figure 1). Like other international financial institutions, principal activities were divided between operational functions and service functions. Originally, operational functions were carried out by the Operations Department and the Economic and Technical Assistance (TA) Department. The Operations Department had functions related to the Bank's lending operations, performed by its East and West Divisions. Its third division, the Project Division, appraised and made recommendations on loan projects in their economic, financial, and technical aspects. The Economic and Technical Assistance (TA) Department had functions related to TA and economic studies on the developmental problems of member countries. Its Economic Division carried out sectoral, resource allocation, and inter-country studies while its TA Division made recommendations on policies and procedures for TA activities.[9]

Box 4: The ADB Board of Directors and Their Functions

The Asian Development Bank (ADB) is governed by a Board of Governors, which consisted of 42 members (29 regional and 13 nonregional) by the end of the first decade. Under Article 28 of the ADB Charter, the Board of Governors is vested with all the powers of ADB. Under Article 28, the Board of Governors elects a Board of Directors on whom the Governors delegate their authority, except for certain powers reserved for them under the Charter. The Board of Governors formally meets once a year during ADB's Annual Meeting.

The President of ADB is the Chairperson of the Board of Directors. Each Director appoints an Alternate. The Board of Directors performs its duties on a full-time basis at ADB's headquarters in Manila, Philippines, and meets in regular formal and executive sessions. The Directors exercise their authority and functions through their supervision of ADB's financial statements, approval of ADB's administrative budget, and continuous review and approval of policy documents and all loans and technical assistance operations.

Source: Asian Development Bank.

---

[9] In 1969, the Economic and TA Department was dissolved. A new Projects Department was formed which (i) absorbed the Operation Department's Project Division and most of Economic and Technical Assistance Department's TA Division; and (ii) created a new Economic Office. Meanwhile, the Operations Department was restructured. See page 12, section on "Organizational Changes."

Figure 1: ADB's First Organizational Structure, 1966

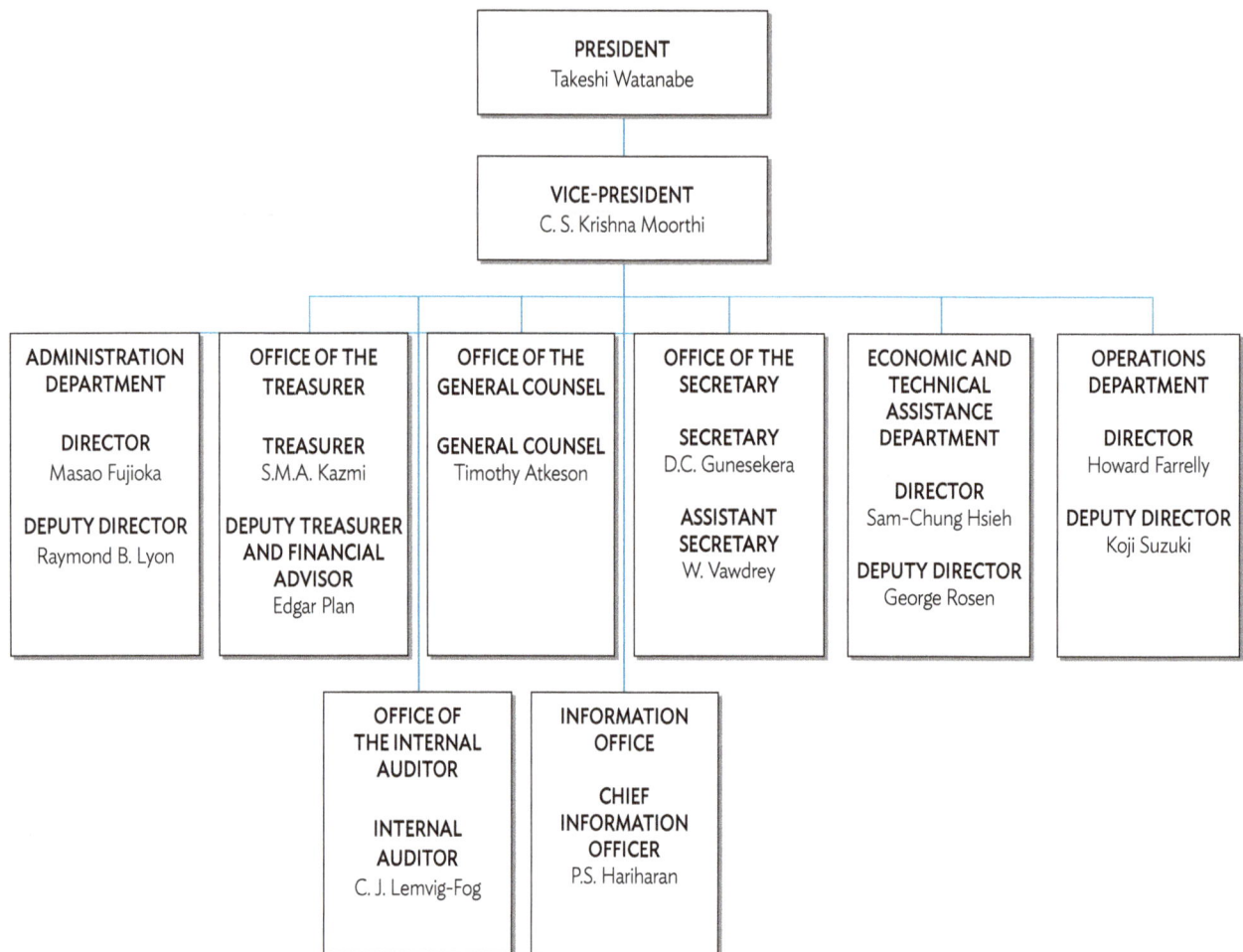

```
                              ┌─────────────────────┐
                              │      PRESIDENT      │
                              │   Takeshi Watanabe  │
                              └─────────────────────┘
                                         │
                              ┌─────────────────────┐
                              │   VICE-PRESIDENT    │
                              │  C. S. Krishna Moorthi │
                              └─────────────────────┘
```

ADMINISTRATION DEPARTMENT	OFFICE OF THE TREASURER	OFFICE OF THE GENERAL COUNSEL	OFFICE OF THE SECRETARY	ECONOMIC AND TECHNICAL ASSISTANCE DEPARTMENT	OPERATIONS DEPARTMENT
DIRECTOR Masao Fujioka	**TREASURER** S.M.A. Kazmi	**GENERAL COUNSEL** Timothy Atkeson	**SECRETARY** D.C. Gunesekera	**DIRECTOR** Sam-Chung Hsieh	**DIRECTOR** Howard Farrelly
DEPUTY DIRECTOR Raymond B. Lyon	**DEPUTY TREASURER AND FINANCIAL ADVISOR** Edgar Plan		**ASSISTANT SECRETARY** W. Vawdrey	**DEPUTY DIRECTOR** George Rosen	**DEPUTY DIRECTOR** Koji Suzuki

OFFICE OF THE INTERNAL AUDITOR	INFORMATION OFFICE
INTERNAL AUDITOR C. J. Lemvig-Fog	**CHIEF INFORMATION OFFICER** P.S. Hariharan

Notes: This organizational structure remained in place through 1967. The first heads of departments joined ADB between 1966 and 1967.
Source: Asian Development Bank.

Service functions were carried out by the other departments. The Administration Department was responsible for all administrative matters, including personnel, general services, and the administrative budget. The Office of the Treasurer was responsible for the accounting system, payment of administrative expense and collection, investment and disbursement of ADB funds, and submission of financial statements. The Office of the Internal Auditor was responsible for conducting internal audits, arranging for external audits, and reporting those to the BOD. The Office of the Legal Counsel advised management, departments, and the Boards of Governors and Directors on all legal matters. The Office of the Secretary acted as principal liaison between the Governors, Directors, and staff. The Information Office was responsible for planning and executing information activities to publicize the operations of ADB.

5.   Vice-President

During ADB's first Board meeting on 17 December 1966, C.S. Krishna Moorthi from India was appointed as sole Vice-President (VP). Although the ADB Charter provided for one or more VPs (Article 35), a single VP was considered appropriate at the time, given the small number of staff and simple organizational structure. Krishna Moorthi was posted in Washington, DC in 1958 as

India's Executive Director at the World Bank, and Economic Minister at the Indian Embassy when he met President Watanabe. The ADB President and others were impressed with his debating skills, administrative capability, and personal integrity, and the President was said to have chosen him mainly for his administrative skills to help in running ADB, leaving time for President Watanabe to concentrate on fund raising. Krishna Moorthi, who as India's representative on the ECAFE Consultative Committee, played an important role in the steps leading to the establishment of ADB. He became Vice-President from December 1966, becoming at the time the youngest VP of any international organization at the age of 45 (Box 5). He would serve the institution for more than 11 years, until March 1978. He proved to be a forceful VP who ran ADB with a firm hand. His primary role was ensuring that sound loan and/or technical assistance (TA) proposals were presented to the Board for approval.

6. Staffing and Budget

The first Bank officials were appointed before ADB opened for business. On 24 November 1966, Douglas Gunesekera, Deputy Governor of the Ceylon Central Bank, was appointed project manager at ADB and became its first salaried employee. He was appointed by ECAFE's executive secretary on the recommendation of the preparatory committee. His role was to facilitate the enforcement of the ADB Charter and prepare the necessary groundwork for the Bank's establishment. For the first few years, he was responsible for keeping the business of the BOD in order.

The second full-time salaried employee was Masao Fujioka from Japan's Ministry of Finance, who would later become ADB's fourth President. Fujioka was in charge of administrative arrangements for ADB's foundation (budget and personnel matters). Recruitment aimed to secure the highest standard of technical expertise, while covering as wide a geographical basis as possible.

President Watanabe personally interviewed a large number of candidates during ADB's first few years of operations. Over the decade, ADB continued its efforts to recruit competent staff. Compared to 190 staff after its first full year of operations, by end-1976, ADB had 760 staff, including two from management; 288 international staff;

Box 5: First ADB Vice-President C.S. Krishna Moorthi
(19 December 1966–31 March 1978)

"This Bank (taking together its staff at all levels, irrespective of color, gender, caste, whether professional or supporting) can be compared to a race horse. The Bank has its owners represented by the Board of Governors and the Board of Directors. The owners have a manager, in this case the President of the Bank. And the Vice-President is comparable only to the jockey whose duty is to get the best out of the race horse, so that it could win the race. I have only been the jockey, and I must remember that it is not the jockey, but the race horse, that wins the race. The Bank, which is the youngest in the family of international financial institutions, has done very well.

"Nevertheless, while it has come in a short period of time to very near the front runners in the race, the race still goes on. The Bank must not falter. It must press on with speed, vigor, and strength. Leaving aside the legal language of the Charter, its mission is no less than that of improving the dignity of the human being in Asia. Each nation has its own path to salvation. That path must be dictated by its history, by its endowment of resources and by the traditions and aspirations of its people. The Bank is an international tool to help them, not to divert or distract them. This is a noble task. In this dreary world, where a vast majority of mankind has to work merely to satisfy their immediate wants, the personnel of the Bank has the privilege of working not merely for themselves, but for the hundreds of millions of Asians who will without a doubt fulfill their destiny, but whose fulfillment can be hastened and eased with outside assistance. The greatest men in history have been people who served not themselves, but others. To a great extent, ADB staff have a similar mission and they should be proud of it."

–C.S. Krishna Moorthi, Vice-President

Source: ADB. 1978. *Farewell Speech*. Address delivered by C. S. Krishna Moorthi at the Farewell Party in Honor of Vice-President Krishna Moorthi. 21 March 1978. Manila.

and 470 national and administrative staff from 33 member countries. A comprehensive personnel management review was undertaken in 1974–1975, leading to changes in the structure of professional staff and improvements in staff benefits. ADB's internal administrative expenses budget increased more than eightfold over the decade, from $3 million in 1967 (first year of operations) to $19.7 million in 1976 at the end of the first decade.

7.   Organizational Changes

The basic organization of ADB was reviewed in late 1968. This led to a decision in 1969 to restructure the Operations Department and dissolve the Economic and Technical Assistance (TA) Department. A new Projects Department was formed which (i) created a new Economic Office; and (ii) absorbed the Operations Department's Project Division and most of the responsibilities of the Economic and TA Department's TA Division.[10] The Office of the Financial Advisor was separated from the Treasurer's Office (which was redesignated as the Treasury Department). The Financial Advisor was responsible for advising the President on bond issues and other borrowings and for the investment of ADB funds not needed in current operations. The Financial Advisor position was relocated to Zurich, Switzerland in 1971 to better keep abreast of European markets. However, in 1974, the Zurich office was closed and its work reintegrated with the Treasury department at headquarters.

The Operations Department was realigned to serve as the main point of contact with member countries. In June 1973, two divisions were created in the Operations Department: one division covered countries of Southeast Asia (Indochina) where operational activities were expected to increase; the other covered the smaller and less developed member countries of ADB in the South Pacific. In 1974, the Operations and Projects Departments were reorganized and the existing Projects Department was divided into two. These changes were designed to streamline project appraisal and loan processes, and allow greater concentration on country economic studies and programs and operational planning.

8.   Office Accommodations

ADB first opened its doors for business at its temporary premises on Ayala Avenue in Makati. The Philippine government would later construct a new headquarters for ADB on Roxas Boulevard, fronting Manila Bay. The new headquarters was inaugurated on 18 November 1972 (3 years later than anticipated), amidst predictions that the Bank staff would soon outgrow it.

9.   Second President

On 25 November 1972, Shiro Inoue assumed the Presidency of ADB for the remaining 4 years of the second term of President Watanabe, who had resigned due to medical reasons as of 24 November. Inoue was unanimously elected as President on 31 August 1972 by the Board of Governors to succeed Watanabe, and would lead ADB for 5 years, until 23 November 1976 (Box 6).

---

[10]   See page 9, section on "Organizational Structure."

Box 6: Second ADB President Shiro Inoue
(25 November 1972–23 November 1976)

Shiro Inoue was an Executive Director of the Bank of Japan and its representative for international affairs prior to being elected as the second President of the Asian Development Bank (ADB). He was chosen for his experience in international monetary conferences, his participation in World Bank meetings, and his service at the Bank of Japan (having spent 7 years in New York negotiating loans from the United States to Japan). He was considered very knowledgeable in international capital and finance markets. However, he had never been on business to a developing country and had little experience with international organizations apart from annual meetings.

President Inoue envisioned that ADB would play a key role in the reconstruction of Southeast Asia (Indochina). Like his predecessor Takeshi Watanabe, President Inoue focused on fund raising, while Vice-President Krishna Moorthi ran the daily operations of the Bank.

During President Inoue's tenure, lending commitments rose steadily from $316 million in 1972 to $776 million in 1976. Membership also continued to grow. Bangladesh and Myanmar joined ADB in 1973, followed by a number of newly independent Pacific island countries. In 1974, the Asian Development Fund, a major soft loan fund for the poorest developing member countries of ADB, was established to streamline ADB's means for financing concessional loans.

During President Inoue's tenure, ADB had to face a much larger crisis—the economic dislocation among the region's developing countries arising from the first oil crisis. In response, ADB's lending rose quickly to meet demands for additional resources including through cofinancing with some Middle Eastern countries who were accumulating "petrodollars." To address concerns over the impact of the oil crisis on food supplies, ADB's lending in the agriculture sector increased, and a greater emphasis on the development of indigenous energy resources became a priority.

President Inoue passed away on 11 July 2010 in Japan, at the age of 95.

Sources: D. Wilson. 1987. *A Bank for Half the World: The Story of the Asian Development Bank*. Manila: ADB; other ADB sources.

IV. OPERATIONS OVERVIEW

- The Bank's focus in its first years of operations was on organizational, administrative, and funding matters. Lending gained momentum in the second half of the decade and was concentrated on energy, agriculture, transport, and finance.
- ADB initially adopted a cautious approach but remained pragmatic and responsive in assisting developing member countries in their adjustment to external shocks.
- To help decrease dependence on oil imports, ADB helped developing member countries explore domestic energy resources as oil prices sharply spiked.
- To alleviate food and fertilizer shortages, ADB's investment in agriculture and related activities progressively expanded and diversified.

A. Lending

During the first decade, ADB's lending operations totaled $3.4 billion, of which $2.5 billion was financed by ADB's ordinary capital resources (OCR) and $895 million through ADB's Special Funds (including the Asian Development Fund [ADF] from 1974 onward).[11] No loans were extended in 1967, the first year of operations. Instead, ADB took stock of the region's economic situation. Management and staff also put a great deal of thought into designing solid projects. ADB was guided by three main principles in reviewing loan applications: (i) the project must be economically sound, (ii) it must contribute to the country's economic development, and (iii) the borrowing government must be creditworthy. Lending gained momentum in the second half of the decade (Figure 2).

---

[11] Including Agricultural Special Fund (ASF) and Multipurpose Special Fund (MPSF). ASF was later consolidated with MPSF. Nearly all of the MPSF resources were eventually transferred to the Asian Development Fund.

More than half of ADB's loans went to Southeast Asia. The rest was shared by East Asia (21%), Central and West Asia (15%), South Asia (11%), and the Pacific (2%). The top five country recipients were the Republic of Korea (16%), the Philippines (14%), Pakistan (13%), Indonesia (11%), and Thailand (9%) (Figure 3).

By sector, 23% of total lending volume was allocated to energy, 20% to transport and information and communication technology (ICT), 19% to agriculture, and 18% to finance. The remaining was lent to industry (10%), water (9%), education (1%), and multisector (0.1%). By contrast, ADF lending was more heavily concentrated in agriculture, with

Figure 2: Lending Operations by Fund Type, 1968–1976
($ million)

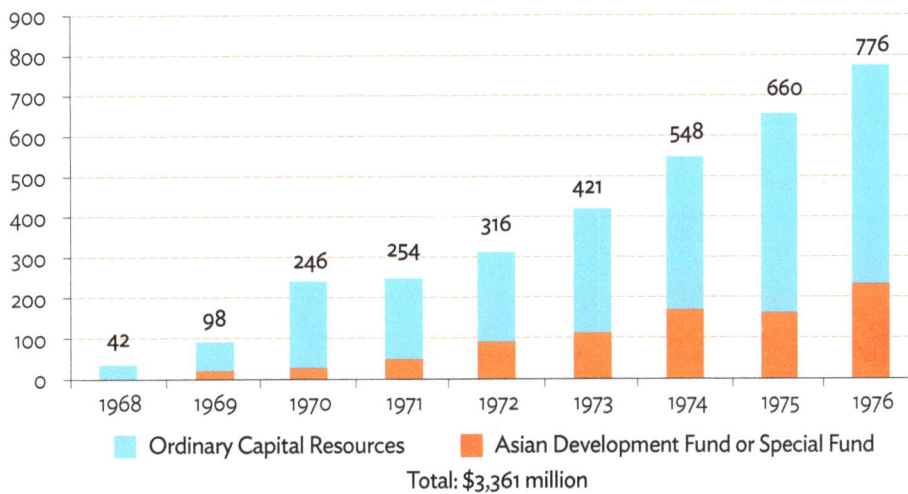

Ordinary Capital Resources ■ Asian Development Fund or Special Fund

Total: $3,361 million

Note: ADB approved its first loan in 1968.
Source: ADB loan, technical assistance, grant, and equity approvals database.

Figure 3: Lending Operations by Region, 1968–1976
($ million)

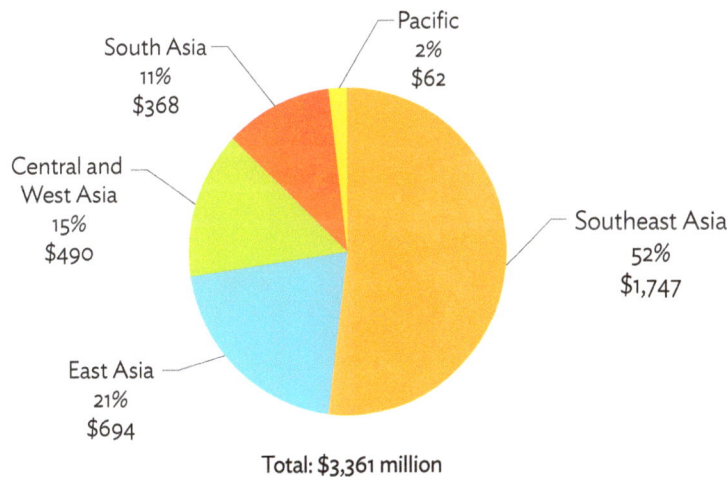

South Asia 11% $368
Pacific 2% $62
Central and West Asia 15% $490
Southeast Asia 52% $1,747
East Asia 21% $694

Total: $3,361 million

Notes: Percentages do not sum up to 100 because of rounding. Regional breakdown is based on current country groupings of ADB.
Lending operations include loan, grant, equity investment, and guarantee approvals.
Source: ADB loan, technical assistance, grant, and equity approvals database.

one-third (34%) going to this sector; while energy, industry, and transport and ICT accounted for 19%, 15%, and 14%, respectively. The rest went to finance (10%), water (7%), and education (1%) (Figure 4).

1. Energy

Asia's most pressing concerns at the time were on energy and food security. Accordingly, ADB focused on energy and agriculture as priority sectors. All operations in the energy sector went to the power subsector. Initially, ADB assistance was mainly for power generation, transmission, and distribution to (i) expand, rehabilitate, and/or upgrade power supply systems to meet DMCs' growing demand for electricity; (ii) improve overall power systems' reliability and efficiency by reducing system losses and load shedding; and (iii) improve access of the rural poor to power via rural electrification projects. In the aftermath of the 1973 oil crisis (Box 7), ADB diversified its energy sector investments through the exploration of indigenous sources of energy to reduce DMCs' dependence on imported oil. ADB energy operations were primarily financed with

OCR (78%) and heavily concentrated (over 60% of total energy lending) in three countries: Thailand (23%), Pakistan (22%), and the Philippines (15%).

ADB approved its first loan in the energy sector in 1969, granted to Malaysia for the Sarawak Electricity Supply Project. The economy of the State of Sarawak was primarily agricultural and its manufacturing sector remained relatively small. However, it was expanding noticeably through the processing of crude petroleum and agricultural and forest products. The average growth rate of the power sector in Sarawak averaged about 15% during 1961–1973. In order to meet the increased demand for power, the Sarawak Electricity Corporation formulated a Long-Range Development Program for 1970–1980. In 1969, the Government of Malaysia requested ADB to finance the foreign exchange cost of the project, which was part of the development program of Sarawak Electricity Corporation for 1970–1974. ADB approved a loan of $3.1 million in December 1969. It was ADB's fourth loan to Malaysia and the first power project it financed. The project consisted of expansion of generation

Figure 4: Lending Operations by Sector, 1968–1976
($ million)

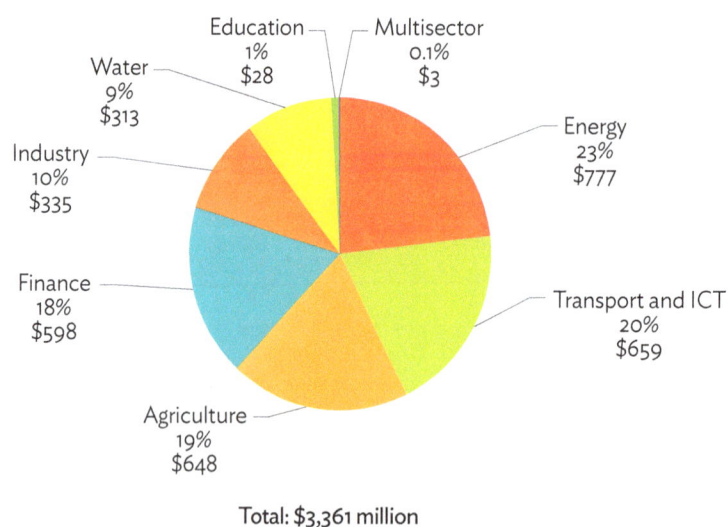

Education 1% $28
Multisector 0.1% $3
Water 9% $313
Industry 10% $335
Finance 18% $598
Agriculture 19% $648
Energy 23% $777
Transport and ICT 20% $659

Total: $3,361 million

ICT = information and communication technology.
Notes: Percentages do not sum up to 100 because of rounding. Lending operations include loan, grant, equity investment, and guarantee approvals.
Source: ADB loan, technical assistance, grant, and equity approvals database.

Box 7: The First Oil Crisis and ADB's Response

The recession in the industrialized world that followed from the 1973 oil crisis brought a steep decline in exports and a rise in import costs—particularly on oil, fertilizers, and food grains—in developing member countries (DMCs) of the Asian Development Bank (ADB). This led to balance-of-payment pressures, falling reserves, and a sharp increase in external debt in many DMCs. In his speech at ADB's 1974 Annual Meeting, President Shiro Inoue foreshadowed grim prospects for the region: "Nations whose growth is now strong will be slowed. Nations still in the early stages of development—or highly dependent on imported energy—may fall back... Traditional nitrogen-exporting countries may find it difficult to maintain their fertilizer exports... Inflation and high oil prices will draw off resources needed both for current expenditures and to support development... Food itself, the most basic of necessities, will be scarce."

The unexpected difficulties brought by the oil crisis proved to be the biggest challenge during the remaining years of Inoue's presidency. Strategic shifts were made in ADB's support to the energy and agriculture sectors. Additional efforts were undertaken to mobilize financial resources, and new business processes were introduced to help DMCs cope with the aftermath of the oil crisis.

Energy. With the sharp increase in oil prices, ADB shifted the main thrust of its activities in the power sector toward the exploration of domestic energy resources to help DMCs become less dependent on costly oil imports. ADB's support included energy development of lignate and coal in the Republic of Korea (Coal Development Project) and Thailand (Mae Moh Power Project). ADB also supported the Nam Ngum Hydropower Project in the Lao People's Democratic Republic (Lao PDR) in 1973–1974, which facilitated the export of power from the Lao PDR to Thailand. ADB's role as coordinator and administrator of the project was particularly significant, as this was ADB's first major regional and multilateral project.

Agriculture. In an effort to alleviate food and fertilizer shortages, ADB progressively expanded and diversified its investment in agriculture and related activities. ADB funded fertilizer projects in Bangladesh, Pakistan, and Sri Lanka. More indirect support was also provided through road, railway, port, and other infrastructure projects to help ease the flow of primary commodities. Irrigation remained a main area of focus to help increase food yields, expand areas under agriculture, and improve cropping intensities.

Resource Mobilization. Under difficult market conditions, ADB aggressively pursued resource mobilization activities, including deliberate "petrodollar recycling" from industrial and oil-producing nations to DMCs.

Business processes. There was a marked increase in the number of supplementary loans, as worldwide inflation led to significant increases in the cost of civil works (rising costs of steel, cement, and fuel prices from mid-1974 onward). ADB also introduced local currency financing to help alleviate domestic financing constraints in its least developed and hardest-hit DMCs. To address shortages of foreign exchange, ADB also started to allow domestic procurement for ADB-financed projects in 1976.

Sources: D. Wilson. 1987. The Oil Crisis, The Inoue Years 1972–76. In *A Bank for Half the World: The Story of the Asian Development Bank*. Manila: ADB; ADB annual reports (1973–1976); Annual Meeting speeches of President Inoue (1974–1976).

---

facilities (installation of diesel generation plants), introduction of a 33 KV transmission system, and purchase of distribution equipment. The project contributed directly and indirectly to the creation of employment through the development of a number of industrial estates. It also helped generate economies of scale within Sarawak Electricity Corporation, thus reducing its operating costs and enabling it to supply power at lower prices.[12]

2. Agriculture

At the time ADB was born, the Asian region was largely agricultural. ADB's operations in the agriculture sector were largely aimed at assisting DMCs achieve food security; and, in the second half of the decade, at promoting rural employment opportunities by providing necessary capital investments. Irrigation was a primary area of focus (accounting for 27% of total sector lending),

---

[12] ADB. 1975. *Project Performance Audit Report: Sarawak Electricity Supply Project in Malaysia*. Manila.

in view of its importance for improving agricultural productivity, including crop yields and cropping intensities, and expanding areas under agriculture. Fishery and rural development were other important areas of focus. ADB supported the diversification and modernization of the sector through the development of cash crops such as tea, palm oil, rubber, jute, and sugarcane. Rural development projects focused on a variety of interrelated activities covering agriculture and basic social services such as roads, rural water supply, agriculture support services, health, and other community facilities. From 1974 onward, overall lending to agriculture increased substantially (Figure 5). Around two-thirds of lending went to five countries: Indonesia (17%), the Republic of Korea (14%), Myanmar (13%), the Philippines (12%), and Malaysia (10%).

The Tajum Irrigation Project in Indonesia was approved by the Board on 17 June 1969. The project was pioneering as the first ADB loan for agriculture infrastructure, ADB's first loan to Indonesia, and the first loan financed from ADB's Special Funds resources. The project was located in a relatively less developed area in Central Java.

It aimed to help the government complete its irrigation system, covering a gross irrigable area of 3,200 hectares. Although the climatic and soil conditions were favorable for rice cultivation, only one crop of paddy was possible in the wet season due to the lack of irrigation facilities, and the average yield was only 1.2 tons per hectare. The major economic benefit expected from the project was an increase in agriculture production and a rise in farm income in the project area. With the project, a three-crop sequence was considered feasible, with some changes in existing farming practices. Rice production in the net irrigable area was expected to increase by 16,000 tons per year, and bring with it a threefold rise in farm income over a period of 10 years.[13] An outstanding feature of the project was the inclusion of a pilot scheme for the exploration, development, and demonstration of advanced farming methods and for the propagation of an efficient water management system in the entire project area. At that time, irrigation systems were crude or lacking, and the paddy fields depended on rainfed farming methods. The scheme showed commendable success and won the confidence of the farmers.[14]

Figure 5: Evolution of Lending Operations, Key Sectors, 1968-1976
($ million)

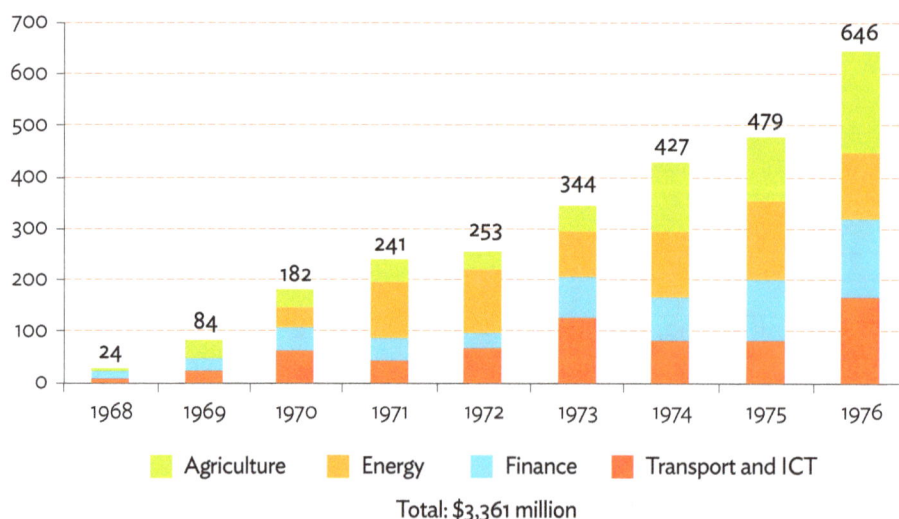

Total: $3,361 million

ICT = information and communication technology.
Note: ADB approved its first loan in 1968.
Source: ADB loan, technical assistance, grant, and equity approvals database.

---

[13] A typical farm has an average size of 0.4 hectare.
[14] ADB. 1974. *Project Performance Audit Report: Tajum Irrigation Project in Indonesia*. Manila.

3. Transport and ICT

To support economic growth, operations in the transport and ICT sector were predominantly focused on roads (52%). Water transport also received substantial support (26%), while the rest was shared by air transport, rail, and ICT. ADB's support in the road subsector focused primarily on the construction of new highways and rural roads to (i) promote more efficient land transportation systems, (ii) facilitate improved access of the agriculture and rural sectors to markets and other social amenities, and (iii) enable closer integration of rural and urban areas through better interprovincial and national transport capability. Over 80% of ADB's assistance in this area was financed from OCR, with the top borrowers being Malaysia (20%), the Philippines (16%), and the Republic of Korea (13%).

In the 1960s, the Republic of Korea was suffering from a major bottleneck in its transport sector. The highway system was underdeveloped, with only 6% of the total highway system or 1,934 kilometers of roads paved. With demand for transport facilities increasing substantially, modernization and expansion of existing facilities was urgent. An ADB loan of $6.8 million was approved on 3 September 1968 to cover the foreign exchange cost of the Seoul–Inchon Expressway, a 30 kilometer, four-lane toll road that served a rapidly developing area in the country. The primary purpose of the road was to supplement existing facilities and to provide an uninterrupted link between the capital city of Seoul and its main seaport, Incheon. The construction of the expressway was given high priority in the Second Five-Year Economic Development Plan, 1967–1971 and implementation proceeded at an accelerated pace. The project was appraised by ADB when it was already at an advanced stage of construction and the loan became effective shortly before completion of the expressway. A postevaluation study concluded that the project contributed to an accelerated transformation of the rural setting, from subsistence farming to commercial production. In addition, reduction in transport costs and time provided additional incentives to generate agricultural surpluses. The provision of easy transport facilities also contributed to a dispersal of economic activities, away from congested areas and toward a more balanced pattern of growth within the project area.[15]

4. Finance

ADB support in the finance sector went principally to development finance institutions (DFIs) in the 1960s and early 1970s, and was guided by two main objectives. The first was to promote strong and effective domestic finance institutions that can mobilize domestic and external resources, provide long-term capital for private investment, provide technical and advisory services to private enterprises, and contribute to the development of the securities market. The second objective was to transfer ADB's resources through DFIs to small and medium-sized enterprises, which received at least 14% of total lending in the sector for finance and leasing. Bank assistance in the sector was primarily (85%) financed from OCR and heavily concentrated in three countries: the Republic of Korea (41%), the Philippines (16%), and Pakistan (15%).

The first loan ever extended by ADB was to a DFI, the Industrial Finance Corporation of Thailand (IFCT), which consisted of a credit line for $5 million approved in January 1968. The manufacturing industry sector in Thailand then was playing an increasingly important role in the country's economic development and the government had adopted various policy measures to encourage further development of industries. The IFCT, though legally a private entity, had been an important vehicle in the implementation of the government's industrial policy. Unlike commercial banks that engaged in short-term lending, IFCT played a pivotal role by assisting in the establishment and expansion of industries by extending medium-

---

[15] ADB. 1974. *Post-Evaluation of the Seoul-Incheon Expressway Project in the Republic of Korea.* Manila (Sec. M23-74).

and long-term loans. IFCT was appraised by an ADB mission in October–November 1967, which found that the quality of ICFT's loan portfolio was generally good, its loan processing procedures were sound, and that its appraisal techniques were satisfactory. The loan sought to augment IFCT's foreign exchange resources. At the time, this was the only source of foreign exchange for relending by IFCT. The proceeds of ADB's loans were sublent for 24 projects covering a variety of industries. Most were nontraditional industries where Thai industrialists had little experience. From that modest beginning, the network of DFIs associated with ADB would steadily expand during the decade.[16]

B. Technical Assistance

Under the ADB Charter, technical assistance is one of ADB's basic functions and is needed to help ADB's DMCs improve their capabilities to prepare, finance, and execute development projects and programs, thus increasing their capacities to use development assistance effectively. To augment its other sources of funds for TA projects such as OCR income and financing from other agencies, the Technical Assistance Special Fund (TASF) was

established soon after ADB started its operations in 1967 (see section V discussion on special funds and facilities). TA operations solely funded by ADB reached $25.4 million over the first decade, equivalent to 0.75% of total operations (Figure 6). Of this, 83% was allotted to TA projects of DMCs, while the rest were funded as regional TA (RETA). TA projects played an important role in expanding lending activities (through careful preparation of projects) and in building up relevant institutions and skills, especially in ADB's poorest and least developed DMCs. RETA was also used to finance major regional surveys.

By sector, almost half (48%) of TA operations went to agriculture, while more than one-sixth (17%) went to transport and ICT (Figure 7). The remaining share went to finance (12%), energy (9%), water (5%), public sector management (4%), industry (4%), and education (1%). Emphasis was given to agriculture in part because of the complex nature of project preparation in this sector, which often involves several disciplines. Also, the preparation of two comprehensive sectoral surveys over the decade was financed through RETA. The top five country recipients of TA were Indonesia (18%), Bangladesh (12%), Afghanistan (10%), Nepal (9%), and the Philippines (9%).

Figure 6: Technical Assistance Approvals, 1967–1976
($ million)

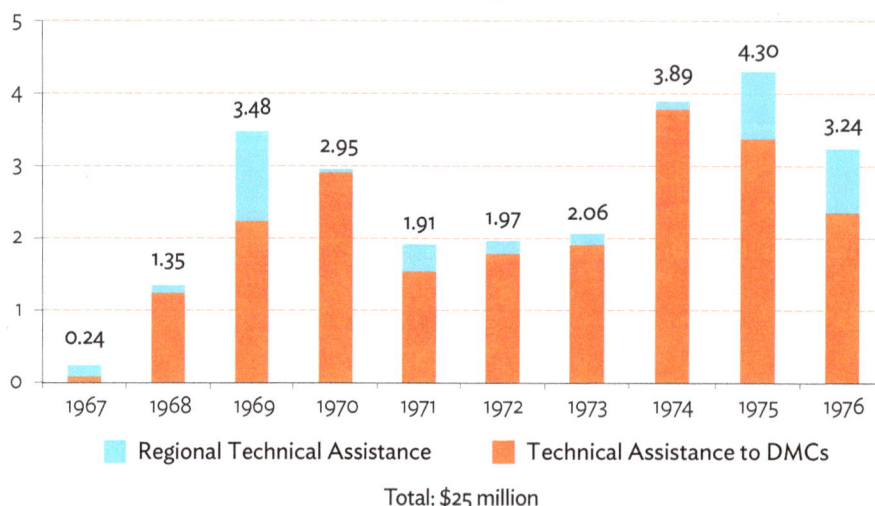

DMCs = developing member countries.
Note: The approvals only cover grants funded by the Technical Assistance Special Fund.
Source: ADB loan, technical assistance, grant, and equity approvals database.

---

[16]   ADB. 1974. *Project Performance Audit Report: First Industrial Finance Corporation in Thailand*. Manila.

Figure 7: Technical Assistance Approvals, by Sector, 1967–1976
(%, $ million)

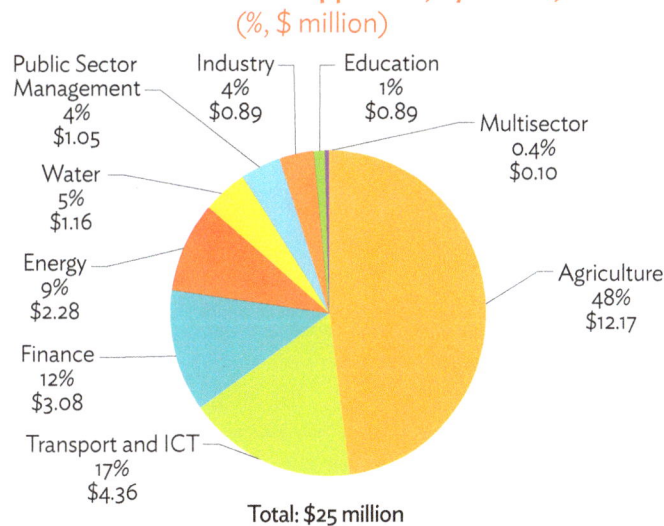

Public Sector Management 4% $1.05
Industry 4% $0.89
Education 1% $0.89
Multisector 0.4% $0.10
Water 5% $1.16
Energy 9% $2.28
Finance 12% $3.08
Transport and ICT 17% $4.36
Agriculture 48% $12.17
Total: $25 million

ICT = information and communication technology.
Notes: Percentages do not sum up to 100 because of rounding. The approvals only cover grants funded by the Technical Assistance Special Fund.
Source: ADB loan, technical assistance, grant, and equity approvals database.

The first TA project to a member country was approved in August 1967 ($80,000) for the Foodgrain Production Project in Indonesia.[17] The Government of Indonesia was implementing a program of economic rehabilitation and stabilization at the time, and requested ADB for a TA to design measures to improve food production and food availability. In June 1968, the government requested ADB for further technical assistance. A new TA was approved (for $230,000) on 30 July 1968. Under the new TA, ADB provided first, an agriculture economist as advisor to the Department of Agriculture to provide guidance on economic policies pertaining to the production and distribution of food, and on the formulation and evaluation of project proposals in the department. Second, a team of two experts (one crop expert familiar with soil fertility problems and with integrated high-yield rice production techniques, and one water management expert with proficiency in irrigation and rice agronomy) gave advice on how to raise food production. Third, a team of five experts was provided to conduct a survey of the Indonesian rural credit system, including the role of cooperatives.[18]

Table 3 presents a snapshot of ADB's first operational activities. Appendix Tables A2.1 and A2.2 provide more detailed data on lending and technical assistance approvals by economy.

Table 3: ADB's First Operational Activities

Year	Activities
1967	• First technical assistance (TA) project to Indonesia on food grain production is approved • First regional TA grant to prepare the first Asian Agricultural Survey is approved
1968	• ADB extends its first loan from ordinary capital resources ($5 million) to Thailand's Industrial Finance Corporation, for onlending to private industries
1969	• ADB extends its first loan on concessional terms from Special Funds resources ($990,000) for the Tajum Irrigation project in Indonesia • ADB extends its first energy sector loan for an electricity supply project in Malaysia
1970	• First cofinancing agreement is approved as a loan for Indonesia for a fertilizer plant in cooperation with Japan, the United States, and the World Bank (International Development Association) • First education sector loan is approved for a college expansion project in Singapore

Sources: ADB annual reports (1967–1972).

---

[17] The first RETA was approved in May 1967 for the Asian Agricultural Survey.
[18] ADB. 1968. *Annual Report 1967*. Manila; ADB. 1969. *Annual Report 1968*. Manila.

V. KEY STRATEGIES, POLICIES, AND BUSINESS PROCESSES

- ADB considered it necessary to take stock of the needs and challenges in the region. Early work focused on comprehensive sector studies, such as in-depth surveys completed for the agriculture and transport sectors, which significantly influenced ADB operations in the early years.
- Special attention was given to Southeast Asia (Indochina) and the South Pacific, in line with the ADB Charter provision for a special focus on small and less developed countries.

A. Important Surveys and Studies

1. The First Asian Agricultural Survey

A major thrust of ADB's early operations was directed toward gaining a solid understanding of the region's agriculture sector. This was not surprising, considering how agriculture accounted for a significant part of GDP and employed the bulk of the labor force in most economies in the region. Given the importance of this sector, ADB commissioned the first *Asian Agricultural Survey (AAS)* in July 1967 (Box 8).[19] The survey was completed in 1968. For this task, ADB assembled a consultative committee consisting of 11 internationally renowned agricultural

experts. The consultative committee was co-chaired by Kazushi Ohkawa (Hitotsubashi University) and T. W. Schultz (University of Chicago). A survey team composed of field specialists in various disciplines launched a series of missions in DMCs to assess the needs, problems, and opportunities confronting agricultural development in the region. The AAS highlighted new opportunities for expanding agricultural outputs as a result of revolutionary breakthroughs from new inputs and production techniques. With proper implementation, these could bring about the promise of substantially increased and higher quality agricultural yields. The AAS provided ADB with a framework for its future operations, and the study was considered to be "a pioneering effort which became widely quoted within the Bank and around the world."[20]

---

[19] ADB. 1969. *Asian Agricultural Survey*. Manila: University of Tokyo Press for the Asian Development Bank.
[20] D. Wilson. 1987. *A Bank for Half the World: The Story of the Asian Development Bank*. Manila: ADB.

Box 8: The First Asian Agricultural Survey

The First Asian Agricultural Survey was undertaken to provide a comprehensive analysis on the different technical programs of agricultural development in the region; identify major economic, administrative, social, and policy constraints to accelerate agricultural development; and recommend investment opportunities, both public and private, to increase agricultural productive capacities in the region.

The survey included a regional report and 12 detailed technical reports on rice production, farm crops, plantation crop, livestock and poultry, fisheries, forestry and forest industries, irrigation and drainage, agriculturally related industries, role of rural institutions in agricultural development, developing small farm economy in Asia, statistical framework for agriculture planning and development, and the general economy as a setting for agriculture. It identified activities that would give ADB an opportunity to contribute to agricultural progress, including support for (i) infrastructure development (irrigation and drainage, transportation, and rural electrification); (ii) expanded markets, more advanced processing facilities, and better equipped sales and service outlets; (iii) credit support for agricultural development; (iv) capacity building to address government weaknesses in implementing rural development programs; and (v) education, research, and extension services.

Source: ADB. 1969. *Asian Agricultural Survey*. Tokyo: University of Tokyo Press for the Asian Development Bank.

---

2. The Second Asian Agricultural Survey

The *Second Asian Agricultural Survey (AAS II)* was launched in 1976 and published in 1978 as a book subtitled *Rural Asia—Challenges and Opportunities*.[21] It covered the agricultural and rural development experience in Asia since the first AAS. Despite the introduction of superior agricultural technologies, the survey noted that the rural population had not shared much of its benefits, and rural poverty continued to be widespread. Substantial gaps remained between yields obtained in experimental laboratories, and those obtained by small farmers. The study examined technological requirements for agricultural growth with emphasis on the interaction between technological change and rural institutions. It pointed to the shortcomings of existing agricultural credit and suggested approaches to deal with problematic credit programs for small farmers and agricultural price policies. The AAS II outlined broad strategies for the next decade to (i) accelerate growth in agricultural outputs; (ii) maximize benefits of growth, particularly for small farmers; (iii) create additional opportunities for wage-paid employment or supplementary occupations in both farm and nonfarm activities in rural areas; (iv) strengthen links between agricultural and nonagricultural sectors; and (v) organize production and trade in agricultural commodities. AAS II also examined the role of aid to support agricultural and rural development, and proposed more program (rather than project) assistance, more local financing, further untying of aid, and the simplification of procedures for more effective aid.

3. Southeast Asian Regional Transport Survey

At the end of 1967, ADB agreed to a request from the Malaysian government to undertake the *Southeast Asian Regional Transport Survey*.[22] The survey was completed in 1971. The survey acknowledged that the development of a sound and efficient transport system, both at the national and regional levels, was vital to the continued growth and development of the region. It covered seven countries (Indonesia, the Lao PDR, Malaysia, the Philippines, Singapore, Thailand, and Viet Nam). For this exercise, ADB put together a steering committee of internationally recognized experts in the field of transport and economic development. The steering committee was chaired by Wilfred Owen (Brookings Institution). The survey made a valuable contribution to the understanding of

---

[21] ADB. 1977. *Asian Agricultural Survey, 1976: Rural Asia—Challenges and Opportunities*. New York: Praeger.
[22] ADB. 1972. *Southeast Asian Regional Transport Survey*. Singapore: Times Printers.

the transport problems of the region. It presented a comprehensive assessment of the existing transport systems, including a diagnosis of their weaknesses and deficiencies. It then presented a systematic analysis on the prospective growth of the region, and projected the transportation requirements (inland, seaports, ocean shipping, and air) for the next 20 years (1970–1990). The recommendations of the survey covered both physical and policy aspects. Many of ADB's subsequent infrastructure projects were guided by this survey.

4. Asian Industrial Survey

The *Asian Industrial Survey* considered long-term perspectives for industrialization and regional cooperation in the following countries: Cambodia, Indonesia, the Republic of Korea, the Lao PDR, Malaysia, the Philippines, Singapore, Sri Lanka, Thailand, and Viet Nam.[23] The survey was initiated in 1971 under the sponsorship of ECAFE in cooperation with ADB. It assessed the potential for industrialization of the countries taking into account the size of their markets, availability of raw materials, production costs, economies of scale, and other factors. It aimed to make concrete proposals for the formulation of industrial programs and projects based on a coordination of investment, production, and trade policies among countries covered by the study. The survey was completed in 1973.

5. Southeast Asia's Economy in the 1970s

Following a request from the Government of Thailand during the Fourth Ministerial Conference for Economic Development of Southeast Asia in 1969, ADB organized a distinguished group of individual experts to complete a seminal study titled *Southeast Asia's Economy in the 1970s*.[24] The expert group was chaired by Paul Streeten (Oxford University), and was supported by 12 consultants from six different countries. An advisory group representing the eight participating countries

(Cambodia, Indonesia, the Lao PDR, Malaysia, the Philippines, Singapore, Thailand, and Viet Nam) provided overall guidance on the report, which was completed in 1970 (Box 9).

The renowned economist, Hla Myint, published a paperback edition of the report in 1972 entitled *Southeast Asia's Economy: Development Policy in the 1970s.* In his preface to the book, President Watanabe lauded the presentation of a cohesive and integrated approach to the problems of Southeast Asia and a common body of information and analysis on which to base not only future domestic economic policies and plans but also future ADB activities and strategies. Hla Myint argued that the existing import substitution policies commonly followed in Southeast Asia should be replaced by a new industrialization policy based on the expansion of manufactured exports. He also advocated policies to reduce economic dualism in the interest not only of efficient resource allocation, but also of economic equality.

B. Key Business Processes and Operational Policies

Consistent with the early emphasis in the ADB Charter on the need to address challenges and needs of its smaller DMCs, ADB prepared its *Strategy for Bank Operations in Less Developed Regional DMCs* in 1972. The problems of less developed regional DMCs were examined and measures were introduced, including the limited use of local cost financing.

In 1974, under President Inoue, further changes were introduced to increase ADB's relevance and responsiveness. First, the Operations and Projects Departments were reorganized to streamline project appraisal and loan administration processes and allow greater concentration on country economic studies and programs and better operational planning, including the formulation of operational policies (section III.B.7). Second,

---

[23] ADB. 1973. *Asian Industrial Survey*. Manila.
[24] ADB. 1970. *Southeast Asia's Economy in the 1970s*. Manila.

Box 9: Southeast Asia's Economy in the 1970s

The report, *Southeast Asia's Economy in the 1970s,* tackled six pertinent issues: (i) the Green Revolution, (ii) the manufacturing industry sector, (iii) foreign economic relations, (iv) the impact of private foreign investments, (v) aspects of population growth and population policy, and (vi) the impacts of the end of Viet Nam hostilities and the reduction of British military presence in Malaysia and Singapore. Overall, it provided a positive outlook for development for Southeast Asian countries if countries adopt export-oriented, outward-looking development policies to foster competitive industries, expand trade, and stimulate private foreign investments. The report discouraged continuing policies that favored import-oriented protected economies, as these tend to reinforce problems associated with narrow domestic markets, dualism between rural and urban areas, and unemployment in Southeast Asian countries.

The report also provided important recommendations on how the Green Revolution, as a major advancement in agricultural technology, could become a genuine dynamic force for economic development. The higher yields in rice required a well-developed system of irrigation, change in cropping patterns and harvesting methods, and continued investments in agricultural research in order to adapt the high-yielding varieties to divergent local conditions and to other crops. The report cautioned against the "lure of nations for self-sufficiency" in rice production at the cost of creating artificial prices (through subsidies and protection) as this may have long-term consequences for the economy. In light of these, the report proposed: (i) establishing a timetable for a stage-by-stage removal of protection and subsidy given to domestic rice farmers, (ii) policies to facilitate the shift from extensive farming with single crop to a more intensive farming with appropriately more diversified crops, (iii) policies to promote far-reaching readjustments in the allocation of resources within the agriculture sector and in the rest of the economy, and (iv) appropriate fiscal and monetary policies to increase both the volume of private and public investments to finance agricultural investments and supporting infrastructure. The report also highlighted the risk of widening the gap between bigger and smaller farmers as a side effect of the Green Revolution. On population, the report stressed the importance of population control as an integral part of development policies in Southeast Asian countries.

Source: ADB. 1970. *Southeast Asia's Economy in the 1970s.* Manila.

---

the terms and criteria for concessional lending under ADB's Special Funds were standardized and substantially "softened." New criteria for a DMC's eligibility for loans from Special Funds were also adopted, based on the country's economic situation, using a prescribed cut-off point on gross national product (GNP) per capita; and the DMC's prospective capacity for debt repayment. Third, ADB widened its scope for providing foreign exchange for local currency expenditures to help ease balance of payments problems and limitations on domestic resource mobilization in its DMCs. A year after this was introduced (1975) eight projects used the local currency financing modality. Fourth, *a Study on Bank Operations in South Pacific DMCs* was completed in 1974. The study concluded that the policies and procedures of ADB's operations required some adjustment and needed flexible application for these DMCs. It also emphasized

the importance of TA and recommended the possibility of a "packaged" approach to lending. (In the decade to follow, during a review of ADB's Operations in South Pacific in 1978, "multi-project loans" were introduced for packages of smaller public sector loans.)

ADB also refined its operating policies. For example, in 1974, it reviewed its policies for lending to DFIs reflecting its experience since its first DFI loan in 1968. The review was concluded in 1975 and resulted in the adoption of a set of more flexible guidelines on policies and procedures to regulate future activities with DFIs. The guidelines specified factors to be considered in evaluating DFIs' eligibility for ADB assistance. It also simplified loan administration procedures of DFIs', including flexibility in procurement procedures.

VI. FINANCIAL POLICIES AND RESOURCE MOBILIZATION EFFORTS

- Resource mobilization was prioritized in the first decade. As lending gained momentum, the need to ensure sufficient resources became apparent.
- To meet the needs of smaller and poorer member countries, the Asian Development Fund was established in 1974 to provide concessional loan resources to borrowing countries.
- The difficult circumstances following the first oil crisis in 1973 increased pressure for an overall review of ADB's financial framework. Consequently, ADB initiated in 1974 its first comprehensive review of financial policies.

A. Financial Policies[25]

To establish itself as a sound and creditworthy institution, ADB has pursued conservative financial management practices, and this has been evident from its very first years of operation. First, ADB capital resources were invested prudently, with investment operations focused on government securities of DMCs (with maturity of not more than 3 years) and time deposits in DMCs' commercial banks (maturing within 2 years.) The deposit placements with commercial banks were particularly valuable, as they helped initiate relationships that would promote ADB's role as an important international financial institution, especially in its borrowing activities. Second, ADB's borrowings from 1968 (up to the early 1980s) were restricted to the amount of callable capital of DMCs with convertible currencies, known as the callable capital in convertible currencies, or "CCCC limitation." This restriction provided further assurance to early investors in ADB bonds. Third, ADB liquidity policy followed a 100% commitment policy (cumulative loan commitments included all outstanding borrowings, freely usable paid-in capital, and ordinary reserves).

---

[25] This section draws on the volume on ADB's history of financial management policies and practices, prepared by the ADB Treasury Department. ADB. 2016. *A History of Financial Management at the Asian Development Bank*. Manila.

A significant development in ADB's financial policies in its first decade of operations occurred with the realignment of major currencies and other reforms under the Smithsonian Agreement in December 1971, which marked a shift from a fixed to a floating exchange rate system. Following the devaluation of the US dollar in August 1971 (the "Nixon shock") and the changes in foreign exchange values experienced by several member DMCs, ADB adopted (in August 1972) the US dollar with gold content as unit of account. In the same year, ADB also examined its liquidity policy. Since disbursements on OCR loans were slower than expected and ADB bonds had been successfully issued in major markets, it no longer considered the policy of maintaining liquid assets at 100% of loan approvals as essential. ADB therefore shifted to partial liquidity coverage, which linked the level of ADB's required assets to prospective loan disbursements (which at that time constituted major cash flows). It was decided that ADB's liquid holdings would be maintained at not less than two-thirds of 3-year projected loan disbursements, thereby minimizing the amount and cost of liquid assets held by ADB. This helped keep financial charges and the lending rate as low as possible.

The 1974 financial review outlined a two-pronged policy approach: a significant increase in the lending rate for OCR operations, coupled with a decrease in immediate borrowing requirements by reducing the liquidity level. By 1974, the liquidity ratio was simplified further by maintaining liquid resources at a minimum year-end level equal to the next 2 years' loan disbursements, instead of two-thirds of the next 3 years' disbursements. Such a reduction in liquidity would result in lower borrowing levels over the near term, but would have significant and positive ramifications for the net income outlook moving forward. At the same time, it was decided to encash the promissory notes of Japan and nonregional members relating to their original capital subscriptions in two equal annual installments. The combination of these steps, and the increase in the lending rate, would result in a significant improvement in the projected financial indicators for the remainder of the first decade. By 1976, ADB had adopted a reserve target of 15% of outstanding loans as a complement to its revised lending rate policy.

B. General Capital Increases

At its inception in 1966, ADB's main source of funds was its members' capital subscription payments. Out of the initial capitalization of $1 billion, Japan and the US offered to contribute $200 million each. The initial subscription was to be paid in five equal installments, with half paid in and half callable. Half of the paid-in amount was to be in gold or a readily convertible currency, and the other half in national currency. The capitalization was increased from $1 billion to $1.1 billion during the inaugural meeting in 1966 to accommodate initial subscriptions of new members. A second increase in capital became necessary in 1971, calling for a great deal of discussions and complex calculations based on various financial forecasts and development scenarios (ordinary loan commitments were projected to increase from $42 million annually in 1968 to $300 million by 1975). In November 1971, the Board of Governors approved the first general capital increase (GCI I), authorizing a 150% increase in capital stock. Of this, 20% was to be paid-in, and 80% callable. The paid-in portion was to be paid in three equal installments in 1973, 1974, and 1975, with each installment consisting of 40% payable in gold and/or convertible currency, and 60% in national currency. The Board also recommended that a further study of the capital stock be undertaken before the end of 1975. The GCI I became effective in November 1972, with final date of subscription of 28 February 1973. However, the date had to be extended eight times (until the final date of 30 June 1977).

As a continuing response to the oil crisis in the mid-1970s, ADB sought to ensure that it had adequate funds to lend to the region. Preparations for the second GCI (GCI II) started in January 1975. A detailed examination of ADB's resource situation concluded that the projected lending program for the next decade, specifically 1977–1981, called for an increase in the capital stock. Consequently, the BOD recommended that the subscribed capital be increased by 135% before the end of 1977, with 10% of the subscription being paid across 4 years (40% in convertible and 60% in national currency). Donor countries responded constructively, but the US voted against the resolution. The GCI II of 135% was authorized in October 1976, and became effective on 30 September 1977.

C. Borrowings

Article 21(i) of the Charter allows ADB to resort to borrowings to augment its OCR. ADB initiated its borrowing program in 1967 to borrow initially in the US, and later in European and other markets. Preparatory work consisted of efforts to secure requisite qualifications for ADB bonds to be treated as eligible investments for regulated investors in various US states. In Europe, the first bond issue was made in September 1969 in the West German market when the equivalent of $16 million was raised in Deutsche mark for a 15-year loan at 7% interest. In 1970, ADB floated bonds in Austria and Japan—the latter was the first ever public issue by a foreign borrower in that country.

Over the decade, ADB moved to further deepen its presence in the international capital markets. It raised funds through public issues, private placements or direct borrowings in various European markets (Austria, Belgium, Germany, Italy, Luxembourg, the Netherlands, Switzerland); Asia (Japan); and North America (the US). ADB also made deliberate efforts to diversify its borrowing by tapping into petrodollars from the Middle East, i.e., Kuwait, Saudi Arabia, and United Arab Emirates (Box 10).

Box 10: Petrodollar Recycling

In the wake of the first oil shock of 1973, the major petroleum-producing nations amassed large earnings from oil exports. President Shiro Inoue saw an opportunity for "petrodollar recycling" and directed staff to explore means to effectively and quickly channel the new wealth of oil-exporting countries to support the development of poorer nations, including developing member countries (DMCs) of the Asian Development Bank (ADB). Among the international finance institutions, ADB was the only one without a capital-exporting member of the Organization of the Petroleum Exporting Countries (OPEC). Hence, its access to OPEC resources proved to be challenging.

ADB gradually built its relationship with countries of OPEC and was able, in 1974, to issue bonds in Kuwait valued at about $17 million equivalent. This was ADB's first borrowing in a Middle East country. In 1975, another bond issue was made in Saudi Arabia for 50 million Saudi Arabian riyals ($14.6 million). Thereafter, ADB made a number of private placements with the Saudi Arabian Monetary Agency, the United Arab Emirates Currency Board, and investors in Kuwait. Despite modest beginnings and difficult conditions, ADB succeeded in increasing and diversifying its borrowings by tapping into the capital markets of the Middle East.

ADB explored joint financing for its projects as a means of attracting petrodollar funds. By the middle of the 1970s, cofinancing from multilateral and bilateral sources, including oil-exploring countries in the Middle East, emerged as an important means of augmenting the flow of resources to the Bank's DMCs.

Cofinanced resources formed an important part of three fertilizer projects, which included $80 million from Saudi Arabia to Pakistan, $25 million from Kuwait Fund for Arab Economic Development to Sri Lanka, and $5 million from Iran to Bangladesh.

ADB also provided technical support to the Islamic Development Bank, established in 1973, to help organize its operations (including through its Saudi Fund for Development) and to explore further collaboration, especially for financing project activities to common countries where ADB and Islamic Development Bank operate.

Sources: ADB. 1974 and 1975. *Annual Report*. Manila; D. Wilson. 1987. The Oil Crisis, The Inoue Years 1972–76. In *A Bank for Half the World: The Story of the Asian Development Bank*. Manila: ADB; President's speeches during the ADB Annual Meeting (1974 and 1975).

Notwithstanding these successful initiatives, the period 1973–1975 proved particularly challenging for ADB as a debt issuer. Surging inflation associated with the oil crisis and turmoil in the international monetary regime exacerbated inflation pressures in western industrialized economies, leading to a general increase in interest rates and borrowing costs. As ADB was increasingly tapping the capital markets to fund its operations, such increases in borrowing costs had a pronounced impact on its borrowing program and on policies relating to lending rates and liquidity. Only with the tax cuts and fiscal stimulus measures introduced in 1975 did the "stagflation" of 1973–1975 abate, creating conditions for a significant expansion of borrowing activities.

ADB gradually increased its borrowings as demands on its lending activities grew. It was in the last 2 years of the first decade that the most borrowing occurred, when ADB borrowed the equivalent of $313 million in 1975, more than its total borrowing in all previous years combined; and another $529 million in 1976. By end-1976, ADB had borrowed funds on the world market totaling $1.1 billion in 38 separate borrowing operations in 12 different countries and 11 different currencies. ADB also raised funds from central banks and monetary authorities. In particular, a large number of developing countries participated in 2-year dollar bond issues, which began in 1971 with a $20 million regional issue, rolled over at maturity.

D. Cofinancing Operations

ADB also made significant progress in securing cofinancing arrangements with other donors as an effective way of increasing the flow of external assistance for relatively large projects in the region. In 1970, ADB participated with other lenders for the first time in the cofinancing of a project—the expansion of a state-owned fertilizer plant in Indonesia. ADB provided support in the appraisal of the PUSRI Fertilizer Plant Expansion Project and financed $10 million, as part of the $68 million foreign exchange cost of the project.[26] The International Development Association, the US, and Japan provided $30 million, $20 million, and $8 million credit, respectively.[27] The project aimed to meet food production targets and attain self-sufficiency for Indonesia in nitrogenous fertilizers.[28]

ADB's first direct value-added cofinancing arrangement was approved in 1972 for the Bowatenna Power project in Sri Lanka.[29] The OPEC Fund for International Development (OFID) financed $3.15 million of the project, while $8 million was sourced from ADF. The project resulted in the addition of 192 million kilowatt-hours per annum from hydropower sources, assisting the continued development of industrial and commercial activity in the area. From 1972 to 1976, ADB partnered with OFID in financing the development of a valley road in Afghanistan; in providing water supply in Yangon, Myanmar; and in increasing fertilizer production in Punjab, Pakistan. This brought total official direct value-added cofinanced projects to four (worth $82 million), 77% of which were financed by ADF. The remaining 23% was funded by OFID.

To further strengthen the impact of its operations, ADB also partnered with external sources in cofinancing TA grants to DMCs. The first cofinancing partnership for a TA was approved in 1970 for the *Southeast Asian Regional Transport Survey*, undertaken in response to a request from DMCs. The United Nations Development Programme and the US government contributed to the cost, with ADB as executing agency. From 1970 to 1976, ADB cofinanced 19 TA grants with funding from external sources amounting to $10.3 million.

---

[26] ADB. 1971. *ADB 1970 Annual Report*. pp. 28–29.
[27] The project however had a cost overrun and in 1973, supplementary loans amounting to $16.5 million were sourced from the International Development Association, the US, and Japan.
[28] ADB. 1981. *Project Performance Audit Report: PUSRI Fertilizer Plant Expansion Project*. Manila.
[29] Direct value-added cofinancing contains contractual or collaborative arrangements between ADB and financing partners.

E. Special Funds and Facilities

From the beginning, it was agreed that the needs of smaller and poorer member countries would require special treatment or "soft loans." For the first 5 years, several such funds were established (Agricultural Special Fund [ASF], Multipurpose Special Fund [MPSF], and Technical Assistance Special Fund [TASF]).

The ASF was set up in December 1968, with a contribution of ¥7.2 billion ($20 million, in December 1998 conversion terms of $1 = ¥360) from the Government of Japan. The contribution was to be used for financing special operations related to agriculture development including forestry, fisheries, and agriculture-related industries. The contribution was to be used mainly in Southeast Asia for procurement of goods and services produced and/or supplied from Japan.

Similarly, an agreement was signed on 23 December 1968 with the Government of Canada with its contribution to the MPSF of $25 million equivalent. This amount was to be used over a 5-year period, on the basis of cumulative annual installments of $5 million, to finance equipment, services, and supply from Canada. Between December 1968 and the end of 1972, ADB received contributions to the ASF and MPSF from nine other developed member countries, for a total amount of $198 million. In addition, the Board of Governors twice authorized the setting aside of OCR to these Special Funds. The ASF was to wind down in early 1973 and its resources consolidated with those of the MPSF. Nearly all of the MPSF resources were eventually transferred to the ADF.

1.   Establishment of the Asian Development Fund

With the need for concessional lending growing, the ADF was established in 1974 to restructure and streamline ADB's Special Funds. Contributions to the ASF and MPSF had been voluntary at the initiative of individual donors and were often tied to procurement in the contributing countries. In time, administration of these funds and the loans made from them had become extremely complicated. A multilateral system of contributions that could be used for lending on concessional terms was needed to finance procurement in any contributing or developing country. Hence, it was envisioned that the old ASF and MPSF would wind down over time, and their resources transferred to the ADF. The BOD also felt at the time that the scale and sources of Special Funds contributions would, unless broadened considerably, be inadequate to meet the needs of DMCs, hence proposed to undertake a detailed study on this subject.

The concept of the ADF was explained at a meeting of DMCs in Washington, DC in September 1972. The ADF would untie resources contributed under agreed multilateral arrangements and be periodically replenished. Its resources would be governed by uniform regulations reflecting ADB's operational requirements. The proposals were accepted in principle at a second meeting in London in March 1973, and were formally endorsed by the Board of Governors at its 6th Annual Meeting in April 1973. The ADF was formally established on 28 June 1974, when contributions to the initial mobilization became effective. That date also marked the coming into operations of ADF regulations.

2.   Initial Mobilization (Asian Development Fund I: 1973–1975)

The arrangements for ADF I were jointly accepted by 14 developed member countries at a final meeting in October 1973 in Bonn.[30] The amount agreed on ($525 million) was to be paid in two stages: $350 million (two-thirds) by 30 June 1975, and $175 million (remaining one-third) by end-March 1976. It was based on a projected program of concessional lending rising from $118 million in

---

30   Although in principle ADF I covered 1973–1975, the actual mobilization arrangements did not become effective until the middle of 1974. Lending before that was conducted principally on the basis of "voluntary" advance contributions.

1973 to $250 million in 1974 and $250 million in 1975. The figure was to be allocated among the 17 developed member countries generally on the basis of their relative shares in ADB's capital. It was agreed that regional donors would contribute 40% of the total. However, Austria, France, and Sweden eventually abstained from the negotiations, leaving only 14 countries committing a total of $486 million. Switzerland made a supplementary contribution to reduce the funding gap.

3. First Replenishment (Asian Development Fund II: 1976–1978)

Demand for concessional lending had increased and it was projected that by the end of the decade, the Special Funds would be fully lent. Preparations began at the end of 1974 for the first replenishment of the ADF. The negotiations proved tougher than the formation of the ADF itself. President Inoue called Sir John Chadwick, a former British ambassador, to facilitate the process. The initial proposal for ADF II was outlined in a working paper submitted to the Board in 1975. ADB sought contributions totaling $1 billion to cover a concessional lending program projected to increase by $50 million annually from $250 million in 1975 to $400 million in 1978. In subsequent discussions between the President's Special Adviser and officials of most governments concerned, it became apparent that the full amount needed by ADB would not be attainable. Certain countries had special problems to cope with in addition to budgetary constraints and inflationary pressures that affected most donors. Accordingly, the target was reduced to $830 million. The reduced amount was accompanied by a lowering of the US

share from 29% to 22% and soon afterward, the US Senate formally resolved that the maximum US share in the ADF should be 22%. The negotiations took 18 months, with the replenishment becoming effective only in June 1976, with Canada agreeing to increase its share substantially. Austria and Sweden became new ADF donors, while Finland and France did not participate. Even with a reduction in lending target, ADB still projected to increase its concessional lending program from $250 million as the first decade drew to a close in 1976, to $300 million in 1977 and $350 million in 1978. Determining which DMCs should be eligible for soft loans was a delicate matter. There was consensus that concessional loans should go to countries in special difficulties, such as those with low income per capita and adverse balance of payments. The top five ADF recipients in the first decade were Bangladesh (20%), Pakistan (15%), Indonesia (13%), Myanmar (12%), and Nepal (11%).

4. The Technical Assistance Special Fund

The TASF was one of three Special Funds established by ADB in 1967 and continues to form today an important part of ADB's TA resources. From 1967 to 1986, voluntary contributions from individual member countries were the main source of financing for the TASF. Because of the absence of a systematic procedure for resource mobilization, member countries made voluntary contributions on an ad hoc basis and these contributions were mostly tied to consulting services from the contributing country. Since 1987, the TASF has been financed primarily from ADF and OCR sources.[31]

---

[31] At the start of ADF V in 1987, donors would agree to transfer a portion of the ADF to the TASF to secure adequate funds for steady operations. In 1992, ADB would start transferring part of its net income from OCR to the TASF.

VII. LESSONS FROM EVALUATION

- In 1972, ADB started a program of postevaluation as an increasing number of projects reached completion.

Initially, postevaluation studies were undertaken jointly by staff drawn from the Economics Office and the former Operations and Projects Departments. In 1973, the Economics Office was made solely responsible for this activity. Early work focused on input–output relationships in projects, using economic analysis, to assess whether the actual benefits of completed projects were commensurate with those expected at appraisal, and, if not, to explain the reasons for the divergence. The first postevaluation study on an ADB-assisted project was completed in October 1973.[32] Subsequently, a program for postevaluation including guidelines for preparation of such studies was approved by the Board in 1974. Overall, 14 evaluation reports were produced in the first decade, all focused on projects, and covering a range of sectors (Box 11).[33]

---

[32] ADB. 1973. *Post-Evaluation Report on Loan 002: First Modernization of Tea Factories (Sri Lanka)*. Manila.
[33] ADB. 1987. *ADB Annual Report 1986*. Manila. pp. 23–27.

Box 11: First Review of Postevaluation Reports
(1973–1978)

In the very first postevaluation review conducted on completed projects of the Asian Development Bank (ADB), 19 postevaluation reports of projects completed during ADB's first decade of operations, particularly prior to 1979, were assessed by the Economics Office and the Operations and Projects Departments. Of these, 18 were approved between 1968 and 1970 and one in 1972, equivalent to about 32% of the total number of loans approved during that period. These projects were among the first loans in the sectors and countries covered. Seven were agricultural or agro-industrial projects; four each went to development finance institutions (DFIs) and public utilities (power and water supply); three were in the transport sector; and one was in industry.

Agriculture projects encountered a relatively more extensive range of implementation problems. Two irrigation projects required extensive redesign after approval, entailing long delays and major cost overruns. Two palm oil projects encountered common problems in the area of equipment operation and maintenance. Agricultural credit lines for specific inputs encountered more difficulties than those provided to DFIs. Lack of cooperation with other sources of supply resulted in oversupply of the respective commodities. As a result, specific targets and projected impacts were not realized.

Relatively few problems were encountered in the four lines of credit lines to DFIs. The projects approved by DFIs were implemented without substantial delays or difficulties, and achieved their objectives of providing foreign exchange for subprojects. However, ADB's procurement provisions in some instances proved difficult to comply with. Some problems were encountered in the implementation of certain projects in the public utilities sector, but they proved less serious than those encountered in the agriculture sector. The industrial project was implemented with no major problems and was completed ahead of schedule.

Among the various deficiencies, inadequate project preparation and preliminary design stood out as common shortcomings. This was attributed to a lack of awareness of local conditions. Greater use of consultants was recommended to improve the quality of project preparation. Most of the projects encountered time delays because the implementation capacity of the executing agency was often overestimated. Field-level coordination was often poor, resulting in delays. The situation was often aggravated by infrequent supervision missions by ADB. Some postevaluation reports noted a preoccupation on the part of ADB staff with loan disbursement and less awareness of overall project implementation. More systematic institution-building would have been desirable in many of the projects. In only one project did ADB use technical assistance specifically for institution building, which was noted as a valuable contribution.

In terms of creating significant new physical capacity, all projects were successfully implemented, although at the time of postevaluation, many were incomplete in several aspects. All projects appeared to be potentially viable in economic (and where relevant) financial terms, although in some cases, additional government efforts were needed to ensure sustained economic viability. Despite all these, the postevaluation reports did not find evidence that project benefits had been directed systematically to lower income groups, except for one project.

Source: ADB. 1980. *First Review of Post-Evaluation Reports* (1973-1978). Manila.

VIII. EPILOGUE

At the end of the first decade, ADB's newly appointed and third President, Taroichi Yoshida, summarized the mood during ADB's 10th anniversary on 17 December 1976 (Box 12).

Box 12: Excerpts from President Taroichi Yoshida's Speech on ADB's 10th Anniversary

"Standing here on this historic occasion of the 10th anniversary of the ADB, I feel almost like the bystander who got all the credit for the home runs someone else hit. The significance of today's occasion is something that extends far beyond the four walls of this magnificent auditorium. ADB's growth, from a seedling to a strong and healthy tree in 10 short years, is a phenomenon that touches the lives and rekindles the hopes and aspirations of more than a third of humanity. It is an achievement that each one of us can be proud of.

"We have compiled an impressive record in the past decade. We have lent, on average, about $1 million a day since we made our first loan in January 1968. Our lending and technical assistance activities cover 23 developing member countries, stretching almost across half the globe, and embrace almost every major development sector. We have helped the least developed countries prepare development plans, identify and formulate projects, and implement them. We have made distinct impact on the region's economic progress by extending loans, which in the words of our first President, President Takeshi Watanabe, combine wisdom with money. We have set higher targets for the future, an average lending of $3 million a day, and initiated vigorous action to raise the necessary funds.

"The Bank has been able to mobilize substantial resources from Asia, Australia, Europe, North America, and the Middle East for both its ordinary and concessional activities. Developed member countries have underlined their confidence in the Bank and its expanding role, by agreeing to subscribe more capital and to contribute more Special Funds. We have stepped up and diversified our borrowings in the international capital markets in recent years. We have also entered new fields of cofinancing arrangements with OPEC countries and commercial banks. The Bank has thus established itself as a sound, creditworthy institution that can increasingly rely on its own strength to fuel its future growth. In addition, we have built over the years a versatile and progressive organization and a special relationship and mutual trust with our developing member countries. We have become a close personal friend of the Asian family of nations.

"Ten years form far too brief a span in the history of an organization, especially one assigned to promote the economic welfare of well over a billion people. What we have achieved so far and planned for the immediate future, creditable as it is, represents only a modest beginning in our long and uphill task. The Bank's accomplishments in the past should not in any case lead us into a sense of complacency. Let us re-dedicate ourselves to the great ideals of this institution and work harder to attain the cherished goals set by its founders."

Source: T. Yoshida. 1976. *Address by the President of the Bank. Speech delivered at the 10th Anniversary Celebration of the Asian Development Bank*. Manila. 17 December.

APPENDIXES

Appendix Table A1.1: Key Macroeconomic Indicators, 1966 and 1976

| | GDP (2010 constant US$, million) | | Population (million) | | GDP per capita (2010 constant US$) | | Share in GDP | | | | | |
| | | | | | | | Agriculture (%) | | Industry (%) | | Services (%) | |
	1966	1976	1966	1976	1966	1976	1966	1976	1966	1976	1966	1976
Central and West Asia	...	...	**102.9**	**132.4**	...	...	...	...	...	...	...	...
Afghanistan	...	...	10.1	12.8	...	...	...	...	...	...	...	...
Armenia	...	...	2.3	2.9	...	...	...	...	...	...	...	...
Azerbaijan	...	...	4.7	5.8	...	...	...	...	...	...	...	...
Georgia	7,539	13,664	4.0	4.3	1,900	3,147	...	25 (1980)	...	35 (1980)	...	40 (1980)
Kazakhstan	...	...	11.9	13.9	...	...	...	...	...	...	...	...
Kyrgyz Republic	...	...	2.7	3.4	...	...	...	...	...	...	...	...
Pakistan	20,696	33,814	52.2	68.8	397	491	37	32	21	24	42	44
Tajikistan	...	...	2.6	3.5	...	...	...	33 (1985)	...	...	...	25 (1985)
Turkmenistan	...	...	1.9	2.6	...	...	...	...	...	...	...	...
Uzbekistan	...	...	10.6	14.4	...	...	...	...	...	...	...	...
East Asia	...	...	**784.2**	**988.9**	...	...	...	...	...	...	...	...
China, People's Rep. of	148,200	244,985	735.4	930.7	202	263	37	32	38	45	25	23
Hong Kong, China	17,964	36,557	3.6	4.5	4,949	8,091	...	...	...	...	...	...
Korea, Rep. of	41,411	113,680	29.4	35.8	1,407	3,171	37	24	22	29	41	47
Mongolia	...	...	1.1	1.5	...	...	...	17 (1981)	...	25 (1981)	...	58
Taipei,China	...	...	14.6 (1970)	16.3	...	...	13 (1975)	11.4	40 (1975)	43	47 (1975)	45
South Asia	**196,863**	**279,010**	**589.0**	**736.9**	**344**	**379**	...	...	...	...	...	...
Bangladesh	22,995	24,645	57.7	72.9	399	338	54	52	10	14	36	34
Bhutan	...	...	0.3	0.4	...	...	...	44 (1980)	...	12 (1980)	...	45 (1980)
India	163,579	239,510	508.4	636.2	322	376	42	36	20	23	38	41
Maldives	...	...	0.1	0.1	...	...	...	...	...	...	...	...
Nepal	3,234	3,922	11.1	13.6	291	288	71	69	9	9	20	22
Sri Lanka	7,056	10,933	11.4	13.7	617	797	29	29	20	27	51	43

continued.

Appendix Table A1.1. continued.

| | GDP (2010 constant US$, million) | | Population (million) | | GDP per capita (2010 constant US$) | | Share in GDP | | | | | |
| | | | | | | | Agriculture (%) | | Industry (%) | | Services (%) | |
	1966	1976	1966	1976	1966	1976	1966	1976	1966	1976	1966	1976
Southeast Asia	...	302,138	252.4	326.0	...	1,135	...	...	...	...	...	...
Brunei Darussalam	...	8,533	0.1	0.2	...	51,008	1 (1974)	1	91 (1974)	91	8 (1974)	8
Cambodia	...	...	6.6	7.4	...	...	...	...	...	...	...	...
Indonesia	57,546	116,999	103.1	134.0	558	873	51	30	12	34	37	36
Lao PDR	...	...	2.4	3.1	...	...	...	...	...	...	...	...
Malaysia	17,276	33,900	9.8	12.6	1,755	2,691	32	29	30	37	39	33
Myanmar	3,916	5,504	24.6	31.4	159	175	42 (1970)	47	13 (1970)	12	45 (1970)	42
Philippines	37,495	64,824	31.9	42.5	1,177	1,527	27	29	31	36	42	35
Singapore	8,170	22,839	1.9	2.3	4,223	9,959	2	2	32 (1975)	33	65 (1975)	65
Thailand	24,583	49,540	32.8	43.4	750	1,142	33	27	23	28	44	46
Viet Nam	...	...	39.1	49.2	...	...	...	40	...	27 (1985)	...	32 (1985)
The Pacific	...	...	3.8	4.9	...	...	...	...	...	...	...	...
Cook Islands	...	...	...	0.0 (1975)	...	...	...	15 (1985)	...	9 (1985)	...	77 (1985)
Fiji	812	1,561	0.5	0.6	1,706	2,658	32	26	25	22	43	52
Kiribati	...	183	0.0	0.1	...	3,263	...	20 (1978)	...	57 (1978)	...	23 (1978)
Marshall Islands	...	...	0.0	0.0	...	...	...	...	...	...	...	...
FSM	...	...	0.1	0.1	...	...	...	...	...	...	...	...
Nauru	...	...	0.0	0.0	...	...	...	...	...	...	...	...
Palau	...	...	0.0	0.0	...	...	...	...	...	...	...	...
Papua New Guinea	2,314	3,545	2.2	2.9	1,048	1,227	43	34	21	27	36	40
Samoa	...	...	0.1	0.2	...	...	...	...	...	...	...	...
Solomon Islands	...	...	0.1	0.2	...	...	...	...	...	...	...	...
Timor-Leste	...	...	0.6	0.7	...	...	...	...	...	...	...	...
Tonga	...	...	0.1	0.1	...	...	50 (1975)	46	10 (1975)	11	40 (1975)	44
Tuvalu	...	...	0.0	0.0	...	...	...	8 (1981)	...	10 (1981)	...	82 (1981)
Vanuatu	...	...	0.1	0.1	...	...	...	22 (1979)	...	6 (1979)	...	72 (1979)
Developing Member Economies	...	1,732.2	2,189.1		...	...	...	...	...	...	...	...

... = data not available, 0.0 = magnitude is less than half of unit employed, FSM = Federated States of Micronesia, GDP = gross domestic product, Lao PDR = Lao People's Democratic Republic.
Notes: Where no data are available for the specific year headings, available data for the earliest and/or nearest years are reflected. Aggregates are provided for subregions/region where at least two-thirds of the economies and 80% of the total population are presented.
Sources: ADB. Statistical Database System. http://sdbs.adb.org (accessed 20 January 2017); World Bank. World Development Indicators Database. http://data.worldbank.org (accessed 20 January 2017); ADB estimates.

Appendix Table A1.2: Selected Trade and Social Indicators, 1966 and 1976

	Trade Indicators				Social Indicators			
	Exports (% of GDP)		Imports (% of GDP)		Life expectancy (years)		Mortality, <5 (per 1,000 births)	
	1966	1976	1966	1976	1966	1976	1966	1976
Central and West Asia	...	...	...	...	**53**	**57**	...	...
Afghanistan	9	13	19	15	35	40	329	274
Armenia	...	...	...	...	68	71	...	88
Azerbaijan	...	...	...	...	63	65	...	108 (1982)
Georgia	...	...	...	...	66	69	69 (1975)	66
Kazakhstan	...	...	...	...	61	64	85 (1971)	76
Kyrgyz Republic	...	...	...	...	59	62	113 (1975)	110
Pakistan	9 (1967)	11	...	19	50	56	210	170
Tajikistan	...	...	...	...	59	61	153 (1972)	136
Turkmenistan	...	...	...	...	57	60	...	139 (1977)
Uzbekistan	...	...	...	...	61	64	...	127 (1979)
East Asia	...	...	...	...	**52**	**64**	...	...
China, People's Rep. of	4	5	3	4	51	64	119 (1969)	80
Hong Kong, China	76	89	79	79	70	73	...	...
Korea, Rep. of	10	28	20	30	58	64	78	24
Mongolia	...	24 (1981)	...	71 (1981)	53	57	...	180 (1978)
Taipei,China	...	52 (1980)	...	53 (1980)	...	...	...	...
South Asia	...	...	...	...	**46**	**52**	...	...
Bangladesh	10	5	13	18	49	50	232	215
Bhutan	...	14 (1980)	...	38 (1980)	35	42	279 (1969)	228
India	4	7	7	6	45	52	226	189
Maldives	...	154 (1980)	...	205 (1980)	41	49	298	193
Nepal	6	11	9	14	38	44	293	234
Sri Lanka	22	29	26	31	62	67	79	61
Southeast Asia	...	...	...	...	**55**	**59**	...	...
Brunei Darussalam	...	94	17 (1974)	18	65	69	...	17 (1982)
Cambodia	8	...	13	...	42	21	310 (1975)	286
Indonesia	14	26	21	22	52	58	188	137
Lao PDR	...	...	...	...	45	48	...	208 (1978)
Malaysia	43	52	39	42	63	67	67	40
Myanmar	...	...	14	7	48	53	188 (1968)	155
Philippines	20	19	18	25	60	62	90	82
Singapore	123	149	131	156	67	71	34	16
Thailand	18	20	18	23	58	63	119	74
Viet Nam	...	...	...	...	62	63	92	76
The Pacific	...	...	...	...	**46**	**50**	...	...
Cook Islands	...	...	...	...	...	...	71	37
Fiji	43	38	48	42	58	62	59	52
Kiribati	...	56	...	36	52	56	161	125
Marshall Islands	...	...	...	...	...	...	101	76
FSM	...	...	...	...	60	64	...	57 (1981)
Nauru	...	...	...	...	...	...	...	...
Palau	...	...	...	...	...	...	...	42 (1984)
Papua New Guinea	17	42	40	41	43	50	165	120
Samoa	...	...	...	...	53	58	...	39 (1984)
Solomon Islands	...	37 (1981)	...	79	52	58	141	68
Timor-Leste	...	...	...	...	37	34	...	...
Tonga	...	27	...	57	64	67	67	35
Tuvalu	...	...	...	...	...	...	84 (1975)	80
Vanuatu	...	33 (1980)	...	...	50	56	128	85
Developing Member Economies	**8**	**17**	**10**	**17**	**50**	**59**	**202**	**135**

... = data not available, GDP = gross domestic product, FSM = Federated States of Micronesia, Lao PDR = Lao People's Democratic Republic.
Notes: Where no data are available for the specific year headings, available data for the earliest and/or nearest years are reflected.
Sources: ADB. 2016. ADB Key Indicators 2016; ADB. Statistical Database System. http://sdbs.adb.org (accessed 20 January 2017); Directorate-General of Budget, Accounting and Statistics.http://eng.dgbas.gov.tw/mp.asp?mp=2 (accessed 8 November 2016); World Bank. World Development Indicators Database. http://data.worldbank.org (accessed 20 January 2017); United Nations Inter-agency Group for Child Mortality Estimation. http://www.childmortality.org (accessed 28 December 2016); ADB estimates.

Appendix Table A2.1: Loan and Technical Assistance Approvals, 1967–1976

	Ordinary Capital Resources[a] ($ million)	Asian Development Fund[a] ($ million)	Technical Assistance[b] ($ million)	Total ($ million)	Percent[c]
Korea, Rep. of	549	4	0.74	553	16.33
Philippines	449	15	1.87	466	13.76
Pakistan	298	133	0.80	432	12.75
Indonesia	263	113	3.83	380	11.23
Thailand	305	8	0.58	314	9.27
Malaysia	291	3	0.74	295	8.70
Bangladesh	11	179	2.63	193	5.70
Singapore	125	3	0.03	128	3.78
Myanmar	7	106	0.52	113	3.34
Nepal	2	100	1.92	104	3.06
Taipei,China	100	–	0.10	100	2.97
Sri Lanka	14	62	1.03	77	2.27
Afghanistan	–	59	2.13	61	1.80
Viet Nam	4	41	0.55	45	1.33
Hong Kong, China	42	–	0.00	42	1.23
Papua New Guinea	–	36	0.52	36	1.06
Samoa	–	14	0.77	14	0.42
Lao PDR	–	12	0.74	12	0.37
Fiji	7	–	0.23	7	0.20
Solomon Islands	–	4	0.73	4	0.13
Region[d]	–	–	4.23	4	0.13
Tonga	–	1	0.54	2	0.05
Kiribati	–	2	0.05	2	0.05
Cambodia	–	2	0.11	2	0.05
TOTAL	**2,466**	**895**	**25.38**	**3,386**	**100**

– = nil, Lao PDR = Lao People's Democratic Republic.
a   Lending operations include loan, grant, equity, and guarantee approvals.
b   Technical assistance operations cover grants funded by the Technical Assistance Special Fund.
c   As percent of total lending and technical assistance operations.
d   "Region" refers to lending or technical assistance to a subregion or a group of member economies within the region, not to any particular economy.
Source: ADB loan, technical assistance, grant, and equity approvals database.

Appendix Table A2.2: Loan and Technical Assistance Approvals by Fund Source, 1967–1976

	1967	1968	1969	1970	1971	1972	1973	1974	1975	1976	%	%	Total
Total Lending[a] ($ million)	–	42	98	246	254	316	421	548	660	776	100	100	3,361
A. Ordinary Capital Resources	–	42	76	212	203	222	303	375	494	540	73	100	2,466
Korea, Rep. of	–	7	25	45	56	65	46	89	102	114	16	22	549
Philippines	–	–	5	26	28	43	73	52	106	116	13	18	449
Thailand	–	5	10	19	18	23	44	37	78	72	9	12	305
Pakistan	–	10	–	37	–	20	39	66	63	63	9	12	298
Malaysia	–	7	11	9	28	24	56	65	48	42	9	12	291
All Others	–	13	26	76	72	47	46	65	98	133	17	23	575
B. Asian Development Fund	–	–	22	34	52	94	118	173	166	236	27	100	895
Bangladesh	–	–	–	–	–	–	22	52	52	54	5	20	179
Pakistan	–	–	–	–	–	18	14	34	34	33	4	15	133
Indonesia	–	–	3	13	32	22	29	14	–	–	3	13	113
Myanmar	–	–	–	–	–	–	13	16	31	46	3	12	106
Nepal	–	–	6	4	5	21	–	3	17	44	3	11	100
All Others	–	–	13	17	15	34	41	53	32	59	8	29	264
Total TA[b] ($ thousand)	235	1,349	3,477	2,953	1,906	1,965	2,062	3,889	4,305	3,239	100[c]	100[d]	25,380
Indonesia	80	230	370	657	220	665	143	1,002	361	100	18	15	3,829
Bangladesh	–	–	–	–	–	–	652	541	924	510	12	10	2,627
Afghanistan	–	–	164	838	329	312	–	250	234	–	10	8	2,127
Nepal	–	101	419	361	242	40	–	140	520	95	9	8	1,918
Philippines	–	430	102	36	538	214	94	161	300	–	9	7	1,875
All Others (including RETA)	155	588	2,422	1,061	577	735	1,173	1,796	1,967	2,534	41	51	13,005

– = nil, RETA = regional technical assistance, TA = technical assistance.
a   Lending operations include loan, grant, equity investment, and guarantee approvals.
b   Technical operations only cover grants funded by the TA Special Fund.
c   As percent of total TA operations excluding RETA.
d   As percent of total TA operations including RETA.
Notes: The top five recipients of Asian Development Fund, ordinary capital resources, and TA are listed in this table. Lending and TA approvals for all other developing member economies are classified as "All Others."
Source: ADB loan, technical assistance, grant, and equity approvals database.

Key ADB Milestones, 1950s to 1976

Late 1950s to early 1960s
- Discussions begin on the establishment of a possible Asian development bank

1963
- A *Private Plan for the Establishment of the Asian Development Bank (ADB)* is unofficially issued
- The first ministerial conference on Asian Economic Cooperation is held under the auspices of the Economic Commission for Asia and the Far East (ECAFE) in Manila with a resolution passed endorsing a proposal to establish a regional bank for Asia

1964
- A working group is established to work on the idea of an Asian Development Bank, completing its report in October

1965
- A draft agreement establishing ADB is adopted at the second ECAFE ministerial conference (29 November to 2 December) after both Japan and the United States (US) express support
- Members decide on Manila as the head office of ADB, and 22 governments sign the ADB Charter (another nine countries will sign before the prescribed deadline of 31 January 1966)

1966
- The agreement establishing ADB is ratified (22 August) by 31 founding members
- The inaugural meeting of ADB's Board of Governors is held on 24–26 November in Tokyo, Japan; Takeshi Watanabe is elected as ADB's first President
- Ten directors are appointed (seven regional and three nonregional)
- The first Board of Directors (BOD) meeting is held (17 December); C.S. Krishna Moorthi from India is appointed Vice-President
- ADB formally opens for business on 19 December 1966 at its temporary premises on Ayala Avenue in Makati, Philippines

1967
- First technical assistance (TA) project to Indonesia on food grain production is approved
- The first *Asian Agricultural Survey* is launched to guide ADB's operations in agriculture and rural development
- Switzerland joins ADB as nonregional member
- ADB begins processing 12 loan applications, mainly covering food production and rural development

1968
- ADB approves its first ordinary capital resources (OCR) loan, a finance sector loan to Thailand's Industrial Finance Corporation for onlending to private industries
- A total of seven OCR loans are approved
- ADB formulates policies on procurement and employment of consultants
- ADB adopts the Special Fund Rules and Regulations, which provide for an Agricultural Special Fund, a Multipurpose Special Fund, a Technical Assistance Special Fund, and other funds deemed necessary
- The first Annual Meeting is held in Manila

1969
- Hong Kong, China joins ADB
- BOD composition increases from 10 to 12 (eight regional and four nonregional)
- ADB approves its first loan on concessional terms for an irrigation project in Indonesia
- ADB approves its first energy sector loan for an electricity supply project in Malaysia
- ADB issues its first bond, a Deutsche mark (DM) bond issue for DM60 million ($16 million) in Germany, to augment ordinary capital resources for lending to developing members
- A Southeast Asia regional transport survey is undertaken to study the needs of transport development in Indonesia, the Lao People's Democratic Republic, Malaysia, the Philippines, Singapore, Thailand, and Viet Nam
- A study on Southeast Asia's economy is commissioned and completed in 1970 by 12 experts; this feeds into Hla Myint's study of industrialization policies and development strategies in Southeast Asia (published in 1972)

1970
- Fiji and France join ADB
- The first cofinancing agreement for a fertilizer plant in Indonesia is approved, with funding from Japan, the US, and the International Development Association of the World Bank
- The first ADB bond is issued in Asia (Japan), marking the first time that yen bonds are sold to the public in Japan by a foreign entity
- ADB approves its first education sector loan for a college expansion project in Singapore

1971
- Papua New Guinea joins ADB
- Takeshi Watanabe is reelected as ADB President at the 4th Annual Meeting held in Singapore
- BOD approves the first general capital increases (GCI), authorizing a 150% increase from the initial $1 billion capitalization
- An *Asian Industrial Survey* is prepared jointly with Economic and Social Commission for Asia and the Pacific (completed in 1973) to consider long-term perspectives for industrialization and regional cooperation

1972
- Shiro Inoue becomes ADB's second President
- Tonga joins ADB
- BOD adopts policies on extending loans on concessional terms from Special Funds resources; concessional loans sharply rise
- With changes in foreign exchange value experienced by several member countries, ADB adopts the US dollar with gold content as a unit of account
- Liquidity Policy is approved, allowing ADB to maintain liquid assets at no less than two-thirds of 3 years' projected loan disbursements
- First ADB headquarters on Roxas Boulevard is inaugurated
- Formulation of the Strategy for Bank Operations in Less Developed Regional Developing Member Countries (DMCs) is started (and completed in 1973)

1973
- Bangladesh, Myanmar, and Solomon Islands join ADB

1974
- The Asian Development Fund (ADF) is established to provide concessional lending to ADB's poorest members; terms and conditions for concessional lending are standardized
- Kiribati and Tuvalu (formerly Gilbert and Ellice Islands) join ADB
- Study on Bank Operations in South Pacific DMCs is undertaken

1975
- Negotiations begin for the first ADF replenishment (effective 1976 and covering up to end-1978)
- The Second Asian Agricultural Survey is launched (completed in 1977) to reassess ADB's strategy in supporting agriculture and rural development; published in 1978 as *Rural Asia: Challenges and Opportunities*
- ADB lending to industry through development finance institutions (DFIs) begins, as a detailed review of ADB lending to DFIs is conducted
- Cofinancing with multilateral and bilateral sources assumes greater prominence, allowing ADB to participate in larger projects

1976
- Taroichi Yoshida becomes ADB's third President
- The Cook Islands joins ADB
- Negotiations for the second GCI starts (effective 1977)
- The review of methodologies for economic and financial appraisal of Bank-assisted projects is completed
- The review of Bank loans and procedures is completed
- Domestic procurement for ADB-financed projects is modified